TRIED AND TESTED IDEAS FOR RAISING MONEY LOCALLY

Small and Medium-Scale Events

by Sarah Passingham

TRIED AND TESTED IDEAS FOR RAISING MONEY LOCALLY

Small and Medium-scale Events

By Sarah Passingham

Published by the Directory of Social Change, Radius Works, Back Lane, London NW3 1HL

 The Directory of Social Change is a registered charity no. 800517.

ISBN 1 873860 36 6

British Library Cataloguing in Publication Data
A catalogue record for this book is available from the British Library

Designed and typeset by Linda Parker
Printed and bound by Page Bros., Norwich

Contents

INTRODUCTION 5

HELPFUL HINTS

Your Responsibilities 8
Mrs Doggett – A Case for Inspiration 10
Raising Company Sponsorship 13
Accessible Fundraising 16

TWENTY-SIX GOOD IDEAS THAT WORK

1. Art in the Park 21
2. Barbecue Party 24
3. Blanket Collection 28
4. Buy a Brick 30
5. Carol Marathon 32
6. Car Wash 35
7. Coin Painting 38
8. Cream Teas 41
9. Customised Schoolkit & Caboodle 44
10. Dutch Auction 46
11. Fast Party 50
12. Garden Open Day 52
13. Host-a-Sale 56
14. 100 Club 58
15. Jumble Sales 62
16. Karaoke Night 67
17. Promise Auction 70
18. Raffles, Tombolas & Sweepstakes 73
19. Safari Supper 78
20. Snowball Party 81
21. Sponsored Activities 83
22. Street Collection 95
23. Spine-Chiller Trail 98
24. Stalls and Sideshows 101
25. Trolley Dash 119
26. Wishing Well 122

ANOTHER TWENTY-SIX QUICK & EASY IDEAS 125

APPENDIX: Tax, Licences, Rules and Regulations 128

Useful Publications 140
Useful Addresses 143

ACKNOWLEDGEMENTS

'How To' books are rarely the product of one single person's experience and knowledge. Many people have had questions fired at them or been asked to look at whole chapters and I am grateful for their patience and good humour. Phil Norton, Solicitor, of Eversheds Charities Unit, Norwich, has kindly advised me on numerous points. His valuable help has been vital in this complicated time of flux in the legal world. Owen Warnock, also of Eversheds, has advised me on Food Safety matters.

Many thanks, also, to my three 'guest specialists', Margaret Doggett, Mick Bennett from Sport for Television and Simon Barnes from the International Spinal Research Trust. And, again, grateful thanks to Dennis for all his work, both on the text and looking after our two lively girls so that I could have uninterrupted writing time.

ABOUT THE AUTHOR

Sarah Passingham has over the past ten years created, directed or advised on hundreds of events. In her work with Norwich City Council she has been responsible for sustaining the success of large scale traditional favourites such as the Lord Mayor's Street Procession whilst also helping fledgling events by small voluntary groups to provide entertainment for local people and at the same time to turn a profit for charity or for club funds.

After leaving Art School with a BA (Hons) in Graphic Design Sarah worked as a designer in London. Later, she moved to the field of professional entertainment and worked with many well known rock music acts. She has also been involved with a municipal theatre, first on the marketing side and later as Theatre Administrator.

Returning to her native Norfolk Sarah transferred her entertainment management skills to open air arenas. She now devotes herself to writing, consultation work and to looking after her two small daughters. Her first book for the Directory of Social Change was the best-selling *'Organising Local Events'*. She and her family live in rural Norfolk.

Introduction

About this book

'Tried and Tested Ideas for Raising Money Locally' is the second in a series of guides commissioned by the Directory of Social Change to help volunteers and first-timers in the fundraising market.

The first in the series, *'Organising Local Events'* by the same author, takes the reader through the planning processes of any local event using a fictitious dog show as a running example. Marketing, red-tape, financial and legal requirements, protocol and what to do if it all goes wrong are all given a thorough airing.

This book and its follow up, *'Good Ideas for Raising Real Money'*, are designed to be read in conjunction with *'Organising Local Events'* if you are a first-time organiser.

This book deals with small and medium scale events that are particularly suitable for community projects, school fundraisers or local charity appeals. Of course many national and international charities have local interests and branches, and many of the ideas will be right for those too. There is nothing in this volume that could not be tackled by any group starting up an appeals committee for the first time. *'Good Ideas for Raising Real Money'* will cover large scale events or on-going projects that require a larger commitment both in terms of voluntary and financial resources.

For the greater part of the book, information has been in the form of *'Recipes'*. These suggestions are only a drop in the ocean of the many, many ideas that are around. You can raise money from anything but they may give you a start or get you thinking in new directions. The plan is to look at the *'Ingredients'* section at the beginning of each chapter and decide if it suits your circumstances. If you are interested, move to the end of the chapter and you can look at the *'Plus and Minus'* section to discover the advantages and disadvantages at a glance. The *'Method'* part of the chapter is set out in a question and answer format to cover how to get started, what legal requirements are peculiar to that idea, how to market the event and so on. Details of legal requirements are expanded at the back of the book along with lists of addresses and books that you might find helpful.

Finally, there are additional contributions at the beginning of the book from 'guest' specialists, as it were. They are included to give you inspiration, extra and specific advice and to provoke further thought.

About events

Most of the events in this book can be organised as individual fundraising activities, part of a larger event or even as part of someone else's event. It is fairly obvious where this doesn't apply but in the main I have tried to indicate where each idea is most suited if it is not clear.

If you are organising an event where the main priority is to raise funds there are two ways you can achieve this. You can cut costs to a minimum and you can raise as much income as possible. Cutting costs does not necessarily mean that you have to cut services or facilities. It means that you cut costs to you. Think seriously about sponsorship, borrow as much as you can and encourage donations of useful things as well as money. Increasing income means that you look at every aspect of your event and exploit all areas to generate extra cash. I have indicated where you can swell funds within most ideas but use your own methods and if you find something works, use it again, but do keep introducing new ideas.

In general it is better to hold fewer, larger events than masses of small do's. Add on other ideas to an existing event, as long as it relevant, to boost income. You only need one marketing drive, one venue, one liquor licence etc. for one stupendous event and you have raised as much money with less effort than asking people to turn out again and again.

A committee or organising group is vital. Perhaps an appeals committee is the best course of action so that you can plan a strategy and not just form committees for each event as and when someone comes up with the time and enthusiasm for a new event. It is hard, I know, but if you do try to take a long term look at what you are trying to achieve, and set targets, you will find that it will really pay dividends. Your group can take a good hard look at why you are raising money in the first place, who or what it is for, why they need it and how it will be spent. Make sure that your work fulfils previously considered criteria.

Remember to look backwards constructively. Don't waste time with 'if only's'; learn from your mistakes and from your successes, even if you think they were flukes. There is absolutely nothing like experience and the confidence of familiarity. Things do go wrong but they frequently go spectacularly well. So remember to debrief properly.

Above all, try to stick to things that you really enjoy. Don't be afraid of enthusiasm, it isn't very British but it is refreshing. Smile and tell people that what you are doing is fun and you will be like the Pied Piper of Hamelin, followed by eager volunteers whatever you turn your hand to.

I really enjoy writing, and right now I feel like starting the next chapter... I hope you will follow me!

Sarah Passingham
February 1994

HELPFUL HINTS

1. Your Responsibilities

This book is a compilation of fundraising ideas that are suitable for nonprofessionals at a local level. Many of the ideas are for small events to which the general public is invited to attend and to pay for the privilege. I am concerned that any readers intending to stage any kind of entertainment are aware of their responsibilities.

There are certain areas of attention that are applicable to all events, be it a Children's Pet Show on the local playing field or a collection of massed bands at the County Fair. (These responsibilities are covered in detail in the first book of this series, *'Organising Local Events'*, which includes information on cutting red tape, how to gain police co-operation and aspects of leisure law.) The following points, though by necessity only in outline, should alert you to the danger areas and show you where you need to get further help before you proceed with your plans; there are brief explanations of regulations set out at the back of the book under Tax, Licences, Rules and Regulations.

1 You must hold an adequate insurance certificate. Cornhill Insurance provide the easiest and clearest policies available to date.

2 You should be familiar with the basic requirements of the Health and Safety at Work regulations. This is a 'catch all' law that is applicable to anybody who is working with the public, paid or in a voluntary capacity. There is a very clear and easy-to-read publication called 'Essentials of Health and Safety at Work' which covers all types of activities and gives guidelines on avoiding hazards and what to do in emergencies. It should be compulsory reading for all event organisers planning anything other than a few stalls in a garden.

3 If you employ fairground rides you need to see individual annual safety certificates. You will also need a Site Safety Certificate which is issued by an inspector who should be a member of the National Association of Leisure Industries. He will want to inspect the site a couple of hours before you open.

4 If you are supplying food and drink you are responsible for seeing that it is deemed fit and safe, even if the public are not paying for it. The Food Safety Act, 1990 covers all food prepared for public consumption including that manufactured on non-business premises. This could include raffle prizes, free ice-creams or a complete banquet prepared in the village hall. If you are concerned or unsure about any aspect of food safety or hygiene contact your local Environmental Health Department for free advice.

5 There is a plethora of licences, permits and bye-laws that you have to apply for or comply with when running events or other kinds of fundraising ideas. I have listed the requirements where appropriate in individual chapters. Some local authorities need more than others (for instance, you might need an official permit to take a vehicle onto a pedestrian area or you might only require a verbal agreement). If a building is licensed to hold so many people, do not try to cram more in to sell extra tickets. The maximum figure is set by the Fire Officer who assesses the number of people that could exit quickly from that particular premises in a case of fire within a deemed 'safe' time. If you allow more than the licensed number to use the building you could put everyone in unnecessary danger and obviate any insurance policies. Make sure that you have covered every eventuality well before your event and when in doubt, ask.

6 Sunday Trading Laws...humph! By the time you read this the laws governing Sunday trading in this country may have changed. However, to date you need to know what you can and can't sell on a Sunday, even at a Car Boot Sale. Some councils do not enforce the law, others pursue miscreants with a determination to rival a mongoose chasing a snake. If you are bent on selling goods on a Sunday make sure that you are aware of possible consequences in your area. Your local Environmental Health Officer is the enforcing officer so check first.

7 In all cases of fundraising for charitable organisations or projects, check, BEFORE you start planning your event, that the benefiting charity is happy for you to be running an event or fundraising project on their behalf. You must never use names or official logos without permission. Ensure that you are not in competition with another event for the same cause.

8 As with all appeals, you must open a separate bank or building society account. You have to be seen to be keeping an accurate accounting system and you should always appoint someone as treasurer to check the finances. Never, never allow yourself to be put in a position of suspicion even if you know you are absolutely innocent.

Sorry to be so dictatorial, it must be my local authority background. But you will appreciate a need for responsibility. Commercial companies have to operate within stringent guidelines for the safety of the general public and why shouldn't you? Don't be tempted to cut corners to save money. If the budgets don't work out, well, maybe you should scrap that idea and try something else.

Margaret Doggett, fundraiser for Cancer Research at the University of East Anglia

2. Mrs Doggett – a case of inspiration

There are thousands of people all over the world committed to fundraising. Many of the things that we took for granted a few years ago such as hospital equipment, scientific and engineering research or development in the arts and sports, just wouldn't exist today if it wasn't for the enormous unpaid army that mobilises itself every year, often at the expense of friends and family, to raise funds to pay for these necessary parts of our lives.

These volunteers are not super-special individuals with charismatic personalities and great status in the community. They are like you and me, ordinary people with ordinary lifestyles who just want to put something back into the world.

In this chapter I am going to tell you about one such person. She is special to all who all know her because of her commitment to her cause. She tackles fundraising in the best way she knows, at a real local level. She is realistic, doesn't aim too high and believes in enjoying herself. Her endeavours bring in about £3,000 a year for her chosen cause 'which may not seem big bucks, but often makes the difference when things get tricky', to use the words of Dr. Ian Gibson from the University of East Anglia. She is an inspiration to us all and touches the hearts of all who meet her.

Margaret Doggett has two garden sheds. One is full to the rafters with jumble. Her dining room is filled with pieces of material, sewing things and frilly wastepaper bins, she has boxes of beautiful hand made candles wrapped in tissue paper under her bed and she bakes mouth-watering cakes in her kitchen.

Margaret fundraises for Cancer Research at the University of East Anglia. Since her retirement a couple of years ago it has become her hobby and her main interest. You could say it is her life.

I met Margaret on a warm summer day at a Hog Fair. They do sell pigs but the main event is a country fete with a maypole, a little arena for the local dance group to do their stuff and races for the village children, and loads of stalls. It is held in aid of the local church but the stalls are invited to fundraise for their own causes after they've paid a nominal pitch fee. Margaret's stall had a crowd around it and after I had pushed my way through to see what the attraction was, I found a brightly coloured stand under a caravan canopy strung with all sorts of hand made goods, beautifully knitted jumpers, cards and goodness knows what. Margaret herself was laughing and chatting, doing business faster than I have ever seen at a fete and all the while enquiring about people's families, thanking them for their support and radiating energy and warmth.

I was impressed, so I took her name and telephone number and went to see her a month or so later.

In many ways Margaret is probably like the majority of people reading this book, with no fundraising training. She worked in a shop. She has a family and grandchildren who play a big part in her life but she finds time for everything. She doesn't have influential contacts and she lives in a neat bungalow in the suburbs of a city that she has known most of her life, but she has the guts to telephone celebrities, senior politicians and well-known scientists to further her aims.

Over the last two or three years she and her growing band of helpers have made their fair share of mistakes but they have had tremendous successes too. Dr. Ian Gibson with whom she liaises at the UEA has a great regard for her 'energy, enthusiasm and dynamism. I have some wicked plans to use her as a full time fundraising organiser' he goes on to say, 'but I resist because I don't want to lose the human touch that makes the Margarets of this world'. And that's what it's all about: individuals helping other individuals.

Margaret is an ordinary person with extraordinary ideals that get results. She has been kind enough to share some of her knowledge and experiences in this book. So take a tip from Margaret and follow her code.

" 3 years ago I tried my first stall. A friend and I like knitting, so we wmade jumpers and got together some bric-a-brac. We made a hundred pounds which really surprised us. We were inspired to do more.

You must have a bit of money of your own. I bought my jumble shed – you have to have storage space, I've even boarded out the loft – and the caravan awning out of my own money. I couldn't bear to spend any of the proceeds on my own things.

Honesty means everything. I never sell shoddy goods and we check that all our things are perfect. To begin with you scour the papers to find where the next sale is. After a while you get a bit of a reputation and people start to invite you to have a stall at their shows because they know that what you sell is good.

I have a wonderful band of willing helpers. At the beginning of the year I send them all a list of the events I am attending and they choose which ones they can come to. I never say, you come to this one or I need you there. They choose and if they can't make it...well there's always another one. I work with about twelve people, including my family.

We run three to a stall. We arrive about an hour before we open and work to make it a really attractive stand. We use cloths to cover the tables, we have boxes to raise things up and we never overcharge.

At a fete people want something for nothing. If I worked out the full price for what something cost to make, no one would buy it. You need to price it for what you can get for it, not for what it is worth. We never sell single items, however nice they are. If you have a pile of twenty they are sold within the morning, but the last one might still be there when we go home.

I think 'thank yous' are very important. We always write thank you letters and I thank everyone who buys something from my stalls. They love it and it makes them feel good. I shake the hand of every person who makes a donation, I tell them what it's for and get them involved. I get a real buzz from it and I love people.

Of course I do get disillusioned by cynical folk. We had one lad accuse us of pocketing the prize money from some scratch cards that hadn't been won during the day. I just told him 'If you had cancer, would you reduce your profit by half?'. You have to develop a hard shell and comments can hurt.

My interest just grows and grows. Dr Gibson showed us around the labs, he is always so appreciative, I know we don't make a lot of money for him but he shows us the equipment that we have bought and it means ever such a lot. He took us to meet a Turkish lady scientist who came over to help. She liked it so much she is going to stay!

I keep my eyes open for new ideas. One of our most popular schemes is to guess the name of the clown. We knit a beautiful, huge clown and we invite people to guess his name. We work out three names by degrees of difficulty, there is always a clue on the clown, and the first correct answer wins the clown.

The most popular side shows and items sold on stalls at any event are the bouncy castles, the band, white elephant stall, dried flower arrangements, candles, plaster houses, peg bags, plants, books, birthday cards – not cheap ones, but expensive special ones – and waste bins. I make those from tubs I get at the wholesalers and scraps of material and lace. They sell for £8.00 each!

We have a Christmas party for everyone involved, Dr. Gibson comes and he arranged for Roy Waller from Radio Norfolk to present the cheque one year. I've got a picture of me with every one of the celebrities who get involved. I love it, it's such fun! ”

Raising company sponsorship

Mick Bennett, Sport for Television

A few years ago I had the chance to work with two of the most professional people in the events world. Alan Rushton and Mick Bennett own and manage Sport for Television, a company that specialises in the promotion of televised sport. You will have seen many company sponsored races, particularly cycle races, on your screens that have been organised by this superbly efficient company, including the Kellogg's Tour, the two British stages of the 1994 Tour de France, and many criterium races. The two occasions when I worked with Sport for Television probably did much to put my events experience into perspective.

Raising money for events was often part of my brief during my ten years working in the public sector, but I possibly achieved much by sheer audacity and ignorance and my methods are perhaps better left in the dark. So it is to the professionals that we should go for help. Mick Bennett, himself a former international and Olympic cyclist, has been kind enough to gather some thoughts together to help readers of this book prepare a professional sponsorship proposal.

" As with any presentation, or indeed any form of marketing, you need to establish your audience and angle your proposal and possibly your event to fit their needs. This will be different for every potential sponsor so you will have to tailor each proposal uniquely. Do your homework.

If possible take time to have an informal chat with the sponsorship or PR department of your target company first. Work out the proposal in unison; it is as much to their advantage to come up with a successful event to publish their name as it is to yours for the extra cash. Discuss their objectives and criteria for their sponsorship activities and see where you can satisfy those needs. Remember that you have two 'names' to dovetail; the sponsor and your benefiting charity. They will have to be mutually supportive to achieve everybody's objectives.

The next stage is the proposition. Show the areas where there are unique opportunities for PR activities within your event. This might be the estimated audience numbers based on a good track record or expected media coverage. There could be opportunities to take the event from the local to a national level. You might be closing off roads to hold a procession or taking over a whole Supermarket to run a Trolley Dash. Whatever it is, make sure the proposition fits the company criteria.

Next you think about the event in detail and usually, if you are going for single, large scale sponsorship, you will title the event to include the name of the sponsors. If your event is already very well known you may manage multiple sponsorship but this hard to co-ordinate and there can be conflicts. The London Marathon might be able to cope with two such giants as Mars and Bovril and still keep the names of the sponsors out of the title but you will find it very difficult for a new, medium scale event. Add a profile of participants to your proposal, especially if you will be inviting professionals or 'personalities' to take part.

Sport for Television always include an overview of how a particular sport is doing in the UK. For instance, cycling is a growth area within the leisure industry and a very popular form of transport generally. Statistics back up statements showing that cycling races have a good following, which means that the sponsors will get good value for money for their involvement. At a local charity event level this approach may not be so relevant, but look at the broader view and if your are holding a Roller Marathon or a Fashion Show indicate how it fits in with current trends.

You probably won't need to work out a socio-economic profile of your audience but a geographic profile will be useful, especially for yourselves when you come to marketing the event. It might be relevant to include some statistics to show the percentages and ages of people involved in charitable events, and how many people visit a multi-day event more than once. Your benefiting charity may be able to furnish you with useful and interesting figures.

Do a detailed study of all media opportunities that your event will offer the sponsors. Don't forget pre-event receptions and post-event cheque presentations. You have a unique double chance to attract sponsors when working for charity as you can weave shock tactics or political angles as well as the event itself into your press coverage.

Show where the sponsors will be able to advertise. Include numbered vests, banners around a show ring, procession numbers or on the winners platforms, time clocks, lap cards, and on officials uniforms. The press launch and the final presentation are all possibilities as is, of course, all publicity. Many events, especially theatre based shows, offer an opportunity for a marketing package to be left on each seat or leaflet racks to be made available in a foyer. Some parts of the event will have significant advantages, perhaps where you have a concentration of crowds; bring these areas out in detail.

Show the time scale that you will be working to. Companies will want to see how often their name will be linked to your event or charity and over what period of time. Clearly, an event that starts its publicity with a press release six months before the show, building up to include pre-event competitions, pre-booking opportunities, merchandising and finally the event itself and all the razzmatazz that comes after it, will be more attractive than an event that announces itself with a few posters the week before and makes a hand over of proceeds weeks later in private.

You might be able to include specialist promotional activities: interviews with protagonists, shop window displays or celebrity involvement. Suggest that the sponsors are closely involved with these areas and they may well come up with ideas of their own.

Make sure that the sponsors know that they will be well catered for on the day. You may not want to go to the added expense or effort of a special VIP marquee but free drinks, a close-to-the-site car park, an enclosed area with chairs and a generous supply of guest tickets all help to make your sponsors feel valued.

Sometimes you may have the opportunity to link the sponsors through the venue or route that your event takes. The Norwich Union/RAC Classic Car Rally, for instance, ensures that one of the start points is in Norwich and the pre-event reception is held within the Marble Hall at Norwich Union's headquarters. A special event may be able to be held in the grounds or car park of the sponsor's main offices. You obtain a free venue and the sponsors are ensured real event identity.

Your penultimate stage is to outline just what you want from your sponsors and what it will cost them. If you offer a choice of involvements you have room to negotiate. Don't underestimate your own value to the sponsors and be confident that you have a good product to offer. If your commitment is a large one and you are sure that your event is secure, suggest a two or three year agreement. You can build up a very productive working relationship if both sides are prepared to sign up for more than one event and you, and they, have the advantage of not starting from square one each time you have a new project.

Finally, state clearly what you will be bringing to the event. Even if you cannot bring funds you will be committing time, energy and possibly many volunteers. State your credentials and your track record. Outline other sponsors and professional companies that you have worked with and obtain references if necessary. Show that you have good relationships with the Police and your local authority and any other permission-granting bodies that you have involvements with – the National Rivers Authority or the Charity Commissioners, for instance. Outline all the equipment that you have access to and any professional help that has been promised. ”

Armed with the above you will be in a very good position to obtain significant sponsorship as long as your event is attractive. There are one or two more points worth making. Be absolutely certain that you can deliver what you say you will and that you have costed everything accurately – easy to get this wrong if you are at the preliminary stages. Say that it is a tentative proposal, if that's what it is. Ensure that the sponsors know the activities of the charity for whom you are fundraising and that they are happy to be associated with each other. If you are raising money for a special project organised by the charity, ensure that the project is well publicised. Both company sponsors and your public are more likely to give generously if they have something concrete to keep in mind rather than just giving money for administration or the day to day running of a particular cause. Give sponsorship a try, its not just for the big boys and it can make all the difference to the way you present your event and whether you make a profit or not.

Accessible fundraising

by Simon Barnes

Simon Barnes has been Press Officer for the International Spinal Research Trust for the last three years; he has had to use a wheelchair for over ten years following an accident in his late teens. The Trust's Officers and all people who are affected by spinal injury or disease have recently been tremendously excited by a revolutionary new breakthrough in the regeneration of neural growth made at the end of last year, but research such as this is very expensive and relies on fundraising on an enormous scale. Simon is in a unique position to explain how important access is at fundraising events.

" Like architects and designers, anyone planning a fund-raising event, to which all members of the public are invited, should, by definition, make the event accessible to all. This means people with prams, elderly people and people with permanent or temporary disabilities.

Achieving this will not always be possible and no one is going to jump down your throat if you have tried but been unsuccessful in your quest. The main point to remember however, is that if you don't make an effort to push aside some of the barriers that face disabled people, then the problem will always remain and discrimination continue, even in fundraising, plus you and your event will be open to criticism which should be looked upon as bad publicity.

I know that an extra list of check points is the last thing any fundraiser will want but as the organiser, it is up to you to be aware and making your event accessible to all will not necessarily be impossible. For example, if the front entrance to your chosen venue has a flight of steps, then you must ask the owner/manager of that building if they have an arrangement which overcomes the problem, like a ramp or a side entrance. I have lost count of the number of times I have gained access through a side or back entrance and although I do not agree with it, at least this method gets me to where I want to go.

If they do not have any means with which access can be gained, you have brought the short fall to their attention and they should feel impelled to make amends. Let them know that they have lost your business this time but if they address the problem you will consider holding your event there next year.

Considerations do not stop at finding a venue where a wheelchair user can enter and exit freely. You will also need accessible toilets on the premises and free movement with no obstructions inside, e.g. steps to refreshment areas. Choosing a public building is obviously a wise choice because all these needs should be covered. (If they don't it would be helpful to all concerned if you pointed out their inadequacies.)

Outdoor events are far from being problem free but they normally present fewer

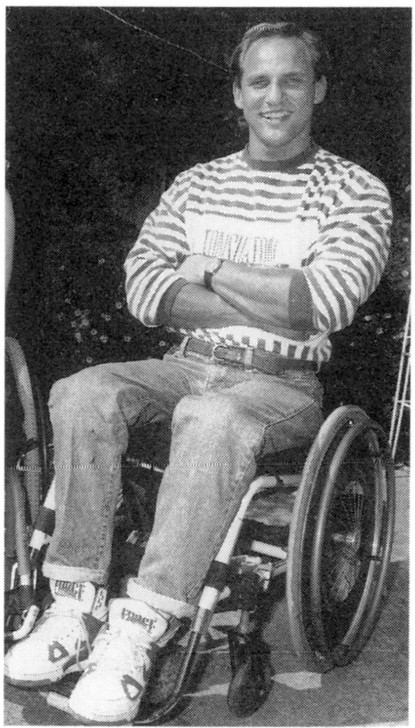

Simon Barnes, International Spinal Research Trust

problems where access is concerned. However, if you are considering a turnstile entry set-up, then you will need to make arrangements for a more appropriate entrance for wheelchair users to use as turnstiles are often too narrow. This will also make life easier for people with pushchairs. (As a general guide, the dimensions of a standard wheelchair are around 30 inches wide and 50 inches long.)

One of the biggest problems facing wheelchair users at outdoor events is pushing across grass or uneven surfaces. It may not sound like much of a problem but consider the difference between pushing an empty wheelbarrow around a show all day, and one with a heavy load, then you will get some idea of how off-putting some venues can be.

Many show grounds have tarmac surfaces leading to stalls and attractions and in terms of easy access for disabled people, this is probably the best arrangement that anyone could make. If you are planning an event which does not justify such facilities then make a plan which limits the amount of moving around between attractions and choose the most level area of your site to situate the stalls and attractions. Again, imagine yourself pushing a heavy wheelbarrow around all day and you should get a good idea of how best to lay out your event.

Sometimes outdoor facilities will have toilets in place but it is more than likely that they will not be accessible; if so, make arrangements to hire some. Assuming the site does not have toilets at all, you are going to have to hire some anyhow so make sure you include an accessible one or two, depending on the type and size of event you are planning.

When organising outdoor fundraising events for the International Spinal Research Trust, we find a useful point to remember when considering the number of toilets to hire, is that wheelchair accessible toilets can be used by non-disabled people but non-accessible toilets cannot be used by disabled people. So if in doubt, get an extra accessible toilet.

The positioning of the loos is also important and what the terrain is like on the approach. In my experience the desire seems to be to place the toilets well away from the action, this can be tedious and hard work for wheelchair users, the wheelbarrow analogy will help you understand why. There is no real reason for this so make sure you give clear instructions to whoever is responsible.

Parking is an issue to everyone these days, or so it seems, and it is a particularly controversial subject for people with disabilities so you should ensure that suitable parking arrangements are made.

Basically, aim to section off an area of your parking space which is as near to the attractions as possible, again with terrain being as level as possible. A simple sign with the international symbol of disability on, and the words, 'Disabled Drivers Only', would be very helpful and demonstrate that the organisers are professionally minded. If you can arrange it, a marshal or attendant could come in handy in case some one needs assistance but a word of caution here; disabled people, like everyone else, will ask for help if they need it, so do not give instructions to your helpers to automatically start assisting when it has not been asked for. If in doubt, just ask.

When considering all these points during the planning stages of any event, someone might say, 'There probably won't be any disabled people come along anyway, so why go to all this trouble and expense?'. Your response to this is quite simple, 'If you don't make arrangements you definitely won't get people with disabilities to come and spend their money'. Plus, having made the event accessible you can advertise it as such which will add to your credibility, but avoid patronising phrases like, "We welcome The Disabled". This tends to label disabled people as a separate group and could have the opposite effect, go for something more factual like 'Wheelchair Friendly'.

If you are worried about any aspect of making your event as accessible as possible and would appreciate some advice, contact your local social services or a disability organisation. ”

Simon Barnes

ISRT
Nicholas House, River Front
Enfield, Middlesex EN1 3TR
Tel: 081 367 3555

TWENTY-SIX GOOD IDEAS THAT WORK

EVENT 1

ART IN THE PARK

A celebration of art of all kinds held outdoors

Operating requirements: Depending how large you make this event, you could get away with one co-ordinator and a treasurer but you might need more helpers for the day.

Equipment needs: Again this is going to depend on the scale of your event and the venue that you choose. At the very least you will need a co-ordinator's base – an open boot of a car, a table and chair or a small tent will do, an entrance sign, you might need some fencing and an entrance gate if you charge an admission fee, and some litter bins.

Lead time: You need to allow yourselves three to six months to set up.

Initial cost: £50-£200. If you can find some land or a park donated free of charge, your only major outlay will be publicity. If you need to pay a hire fee you will have to work out your budget very carefully to see if this event is worth the price. On the other hand it is an attractive idea and good for sponsorship.

Suitable for: Fundraising for hospitals, art centres, community groups, schools, colleges, rag-week at universities, children's organisations and other city or town based groups. Probably not right for holding in the country unless as specifically part of a rural art scheme.

Expected return: If you are charging an entrance fee you might expect over £250 but if your main way of raising funds is to hold a collection, your proceeds might be less. You will need to weigh up your location versus your audience. A city-centre park will attract crowds of casual shoppers and they may be willing to give to a collection and pay a small fee for individual activities, but would be less happy at being charged an entrance fee as their time is limited. A university campus based event may be better off charging admission but leaving all the attractions free of charge; you could also charge for parking as space and helping hands are not at a premium.

What's in it for the contributors: You are offering a bright, colourful, busy event that appeals to all ages. People have a chance to show off their talents and creativity and many will welcome an opportunity to learn or try out something new.

Frequency: For the casual low-key event you could be looking at a once-a-week exhibition from art exhibitors all contributing a percentage of sales. For a larger scale event you will be restricted to an annual show.

Special requirements: If you are including music as a major feature of your show you may need to apply for a Public Entertainment Licence from your local authority. If you include a booze tent you will need a Liquor Licence from the local magistrates court and if you include food, other than tea and buns, you will need to get advice from your local Environmental Health department to ensure that you comply with the current Food Safety Acts. You may also need a collection permit if you intend to rattle tins at visitors: this is also available from your local council. Think seriously about obtaining insurance cover especially if you might be including something potentially dangerous such as fire-eating.

Variations on a theme: Sculpture exhibition. Open air painting sale.

> **HANDY HINT**
>
> If you have a city centre location, advertise on the day by using a couple of people dressed up to drum up trade from the main shopping areas. Erect a few direction signs to ensure that interested people can find their way easily.

What is Art in the Park?

As the name implies, it is a collection of artistic (I use the term loosely) endeavours all taking place in the open air. Some aspects may consist of an artist selling work on a stall or stand. Other areas might include teaching people to juggle or letting them try their luck at unicycling. You might charge people to listen to an open air concert or you might have a band in a bandstand adding to the atmosphere. One event I organised included hourly kite-making and origami workshops. The 'how-to' leaflets were an additional and popular source of income. Another popular and rather more serious activity would be to have an exhibition of sculpture in the open. Not a lot of scope for fundraising there but you could apply for a grant from your regional Arts Board or try to get sponsorship from a local company or local branch of a national company, and then sell literature to go with it or make a collection.

So how do I raise money from this event?

Decide if you will work on an entrance fee basis. This is only possible if your area is adequately fenced. Think about charging for car parking. Consider a collection or donation boxes. For a long term display or exhibition you could protect your boxes permanently within a brick pillar. You could charge a fee for commercial stall pitches. Or ask for a percentage of the take from amateurs, but since you cannot keep control of this type of payment you are really asking stall holders to make a donation if they have had a good day. Volunteers might be prepared to club together over the preceding weeks and make things to sell. Volunteers with special skills can offer workshops or trial sessions (at a price) in circus skills, face painting, cycle and splatter painting – a la Jackson Pollock, no-fire pottery, you name it, the list is endless.

How do I get started?

Form a group or committee. Work out your venue and the type of show you wish to promote then check that your benefiting charity are happy for you to use this idea.

Contact the local college or Art School well in advance and enquire if they would be interested to design posters and organise the printing as part of their course work. This approach is often very successful as students are usually delighted to be working on something 'for real'. You may have to contribute towards the cost of paper as education establishments are frequently as strapped for cash as you are.

Try to make a decision as to whether you are going for serious art and high culture or if you are just organising a bit of fun. It is probably best not to mix the two as you might trivialise artists' work on the one hand or become too elitist on the other.

If you are going for the serious angle, consider contacting your Regional Arts Board and asking their advice. They may well be able to put you in touch with local artists, give financial aid or assist in the marketing. This approach is particularly relevant if you are fundraising for an arts organisation.

Prepare your marketing plan according to the style of your event and your potential audience and put your publicity where the right people will see it. Try not to use the scatter-gun approach. It wastes money and materials and is not effective.

Possible problems?

Local residents or shops may take a dim view if you are noisy or they perceive competition. If you irritate people you may not be able to hold the event again, so be considerate. Find out what legal requirements you need to cover before you plan your contents. Someone else may have booked the same collection day or the park you have chosen might be barred from holding events requiring a Public Entertainment Licence.

PLUS & MINUS

- ⊞ Very flexible event
- ⊞ Very atmospheric
- ⊞ Family event
- ⊞ Excellent PR for arts groups
- ⊟ Can get a bit out of hand unless strictly controlled
- ⊟ Not a great money spinner for the work involved
- ⊟ Relies on good weather unless you hold sensitive areas in a marquee
- ⊟ You might need to apply for licences well in advance

EVENT 2 BARBECUE PARTY

Selling food cooked outside.

Operating requirements: Small committee consisting of co-ordinator, treasurer, publicist and 'head chef'. Consider asking someone to be in charge of arranging some entertainment for children.

Equipment needs: Venue, commercial barbecue, fuel, fire lighters or fluid, cooking utensils, plates and cutlery – disposable or otherwise, food and drink, tickets, a few tables and chairs, plenty of fresh water, means of keeping food cool and lights, if you are planning an evening event.

Lead time: 2 or 3 months.

Initial cost: Allow 50p – 75p per head for food and 20p for a soft drink. Food would include a burger in a bun or a vegiburger or a drumstick, some sauce and salad. If you plan to make it simpler or to add ice cream or lollies, adjust the price accordingly. Do not over-cater. Tickets will cost you about £25 and you must not forget advertising costs.

Suitable for: Local or national appeals.

Expected return: If you sell everything you should make three or four times your initial outlay.

What's in it for supporters: A chance to get involved with a local cause, meet friends and have a bit of a party.

Frequency: One-off.

Special requirements: You need to be aware of the Food Safety Act, 1990. The regulations covering the selling or supplying of food cover everyone preparing food other than in a domestic situation. If you were found to be supplying unfit food, even for charity or gratis you would still be liable for prosecution. Read all the government guidelines carefully or persuade someone in the catering business to organise the cooking side of your barbecue for you. If you plan to have a bar you will need to apply for a Liquor Licence.

Variations on a theme: A beach party. Vegetarian food. Historical fancy dress, try Neanderthal man! Have a 'cook- out' from the Wild West. Try a night-time barbecue or mix any of the above. Giant hardboard cacti floodlit from below would give a quick and impressive atmospheric touch. You could even throw a posh cocktail party with barbecued nibbles; especially good if you have a large and impressive setting.

How does it work?

Basically you are selling barbecued food for profit in a party atmosphere. There are probably many ways of organising a barbecue, but you really need to choose a system that will be safe, fun and won't leave you with plates of wasted food.

The simplest method to ensure that you achieve all three is to hold the event at midday, in a large private garden with access to a fridge, running water and loos. If there is a large garage or barn to actually cook the food in if it turns wet, so much the better. Spread the word amongst friends and the local community, lay on some entertainment for children and sell tickets in advance.

Once you have sold your tickets you will know how many children and adults to cater for, give or take a few latecomers. You will have cash in hand to buy your essentials and will be in a position to ask for discounts if you intend to feed fifty or over.

How do we get started?

Decide on your venue and a date. Choose a venue that has a firm flat space for the cooking area, preferably sheltered from the wind. Watch for overhanging branches or vegetation and set up your grills well away from danger. Consider holding barbecues out of the usual summer period. Hot food is equally welcome on bonfire-night or even in the snow!

Get two or three quotes from local suppliers to give you an idea of what your costs will be per head. If you can ask friends and helpers to donate some of the food, so much the better. Reckon to sell at least fifty tickets, hopefully you will do more, and make enquiries at the time with regard to obtaining a large commercial barbecue. Some butchers are prepared to hire these at a nominal rate or even free of charge if you buy enough from them. Don't try to make do with domestic barbecues, they won't stay at a constant heat for long enough and you will still be cooking when the sun goes down. Look in the yellow pages for a gas barbecue if you are desperate.

Decide if you need some entertainment for youngsters, a bouncy castle, a magic show, or perhaps every participating family could agree to bring a bike or a ride-on toy, maybe there already is a sand pit or you could provide a story corner. If you expect very young children ensure that dangerous areas such as sheds, farm animals, ditches or ponds and roads are inaccessible.

As soon as you are sure of your budget (restaurants tend to treble or quadruple the cost of ingredients to arrive at the sale price), get your tickets printed. Remember to publish the date and time, the address, the appeal and what is included in the price. Tickets will probably work out to about £2/£3 for adults and about £1.50 for children. They should include one plateful of food and one soft drink. If people would like more they have to pay extra for it. And if you want to include a cash bar you will need to apply for a Liquor Licence at least three months before the date, although people could bring their own booze.

HANDY HINT

For the purposes of budgeting allow 6 glasses of wine or orange juice from a 70cl bottle and 8 glasses from 1 litre. Beer and lager is obviously sold by the pint and half pint or by the can. It is probably better not to sell spirits at all at a lunch time party.

Advertise your event by asking your children or grandchildren to colour photocopied A4 posters. Display them in local shops, pubs, community halls or leisure centres. Run a paragraph or a small ad in the Parish magazine or community news. If you ask as many friends as you can to each sell ten tickets, you should have a good crowd in any case.

Plan to supply a few picnic tables and chairs for those who find it very uncomfortable sitting on the ground, but in my experience you really don't need to worry much about seating arrangements, people often bring their own or stand about in groups.

Make sure you think about a car park or tell people where they cannot park. For a big party and where visitors are unfamiliar with the house and garden, make a few signs to point the way to the car park, toilets or entertainment. You might need to hire a mobile loo if you expect a good crowd.

How do we cook the food safely?

Try to avoid buying frozen food. If you have to freeze it yourselves or you have no option other than to buy pre-frozen make sure that you defrost very thoroughly in a fridge for 24 hours.

Some people advocate pre-cooking food. You really need not pre-cook burgers. In some cases the act of cooling the food and re-heating is more dangerous than cooking it from the raw. Caterers will occasionally cook drumsticks or chicken joints in boiling salted water prior to

SIMPLE GUIDELINES FOR BARBECUES

- Use clean utensils and equipment.
- Make sure that you wash them frequently and that you have separate facilities for washing hands.
- You need an adequate supply of hot and cold water.
- A thermometer is recommended to check the temperatures of cooked food.
- Make sure that your barbecue is really hot. Ideally you should light the charcoal 1 hour before you use it. After 20 minutes rake the embers into an even layer, cover with more charcoal and leave for another 30-40 minutes to ensure there are no cold spots.
- Keep all raw food as cool as possible and eat cooked food as soon as it is ready.
- Ensure that food is thoroughly cooked all through, use thin cuts where possible.
- As soon as you finish cooking remove the grills to prevent grease from becoming burnt on.
- Do not transport the barbecue until it is absolutely cold.
- Always follow the Golden Rules for food hygiene as outlined in the government produced Food Sense booklet No. PB0351.

Barbecues have been known to blow over in strong winds or be knocked over, so keep the general public away from the cooking area as far as possible.

barbecueing; but again, you must cool your meat quickly and keep it below 4° C before you heat it again.

How do we organise the day itself?

Prepare salads the evening before, or in the morning if you have lots of helpers. Collect the meat at the last minute, unless you are pre-cooking, so that you don't have to worry about keeping quantities of raw meat cool in a domestic fridge. Keep stocks in a cool box beside the barbecue so that you can cook as it is ordered. For that special touch make up a large pan of barbecue sauce. It is inexpensive to make and really adds a home-cooked feel to the meal.

Put out trestle tables with paper plates, paper napkins and plastic cutlery, salads and sauces if you are using them. Have a clean dustbin with a liner nearby for rubbish. Use a separate table for drinks, in plastic or paper cups. Tickets are exchanged for a plate of food and a drink. To prevent accidents and crowding make sure that there are enough helpers to serve the food. Keep the cooking area behind the serving tables and you shouldn't have a problem. Extra hungry people can buy second helpings by paying the servers; in this way you wont be dropping coins onto the barbecue and the cooks won't be forced to handle grubby money.

If you put a start and a finish time on the tickets, say, twelve o'clock 'till three, people will come in dribs and drabs and you should be able to cope with the demand. If you only publish the start time you may find you have a huge crowd at the beginning and too many hungry people to feed within a reasonable time. Try to keep tabs on how many tickets have been redeemed (clip them into bundles of ten) and you should be able to judge how much more you should be cooking as you come to the end.

You could swell your funds by holding a raffle or a tombola or by selling tea and coffee.

As the last satisfied customers are going, collect all the rubbish and plates of any uneaten food, tie them into black bin liners and, unless you have a rubbish collection within 24 hours, take them to a tip or you will attract vermin.

Remember to publish your proceeds so that the people who supported you can see the results of your efforts. If you have a large cheque to hand over to a national charity extend your PR by having an official presentation with local media present.

PLUS & MINUS

- \+ Good, popular, family event.
- \+ No need to hire a venue.
- \+ Sell tickets in advance so cash in hand for initial outlay.
- \+ Can budget fairly accurately.
- \+ No need to supply chairs etc.
- \+ No expensive advertising needed.
- − Reliant on good weather.
- − Do need a reliable barbecue.
- − Quite labour intensive.
- − Potentially risky way of cooking food, although no problem if you are sensible and study some basic guidelines.

BLANKET COLLECTION

Spectators throw money into a moving blanket

Operating requirements: Co-ordinator, treasurer. 12 helpers.

Equipment needs: 2 large, not too good, strong blankets.

Lead time: A couple of weeks, but in practice you will need as long as it takes to find the right venue.

Initial cost: Nil.

Suitable for: Local and human interest appeals.

Expected return: Over a hundred pounds.

What's in it for contributors: Instant amusement, following the crowd.

Frequency: Any sporting event.

How does it work?

Two teams running around the perimeter of a playing area, usually a football pitch, catch money thrown into the blanket from the crowd.

How do we get started?

Everything hangs on the agreement of the 'powers-that-be' allowing you to belt round a pitch exploiting their audience.

The obvious place to try first is the local football club. You could also try any other arena-held sports meeting. Aim for a date where a large crowd is expected and ask to take the blanket round at half time, when the crowds are excited but not leaving to go home.

For safety's sake you should also arrange for a private room where you can sort the money, count it and bag it prior to banking it. As the sporting event may well take place on a Saturday or in the evening you might need permission to store the money in a safe on the premises until a more convenient time. If you have completed your count by the end of the match, announce the figure collected.

HANDY HINT

Use old sheets instead of a blanket and paint the charity logo in the middle.

How do we get the most from this idea?

Inform the commentators all about your appeal and your target figure. Ask them to announce your cause and with any luck they will keep encouraging the crowd to contribute.

Arrange two teams to travel round the pitch, one team travelling clockwise, the other anticlockwise, thereby getting two bites at the same cherry. Use four people for the corners of each blanket and two to follow behind picking up all the coins that didn't quite make it. You could arrange a bucket collection at the same time along the back rows to maximise the potential and organise another collection at the exits when the match finishes.

You can liven the activity up a little and prolong the collection potential by marching to music and including a band to parade at the same time. If you have trouble obtaining a live band you might be able to persuade the commentator to play some music over the PA systems.

Do we need a Public Collection Licence?

Well, as stated at the beginning of the book, we are in a state of flux where it comes to new acts and laws covering this area. Regulations should be published by the end of 1994 so we shall all be a little clearer by then. Certainly a football ground during the course of a match used to be exempted under the grounds of the previous regulations and general agreement is that it will remain so by virtue of the fact that access to the ground has only been granted because of payment for a ticket. It has been specifically stated that interiors of shops and theatres are to be exempted from the need to obtain a licence and I feel that a football ground will be treated in the same way. But if you are in any doubt, contact the Licensing Department of your local authority.

Possible problems

Flying coins can hurt and could be dangerous. Suggest that your teams wear fancy dress and cover their heads, alternatively they could all wear hard hats.

PLUS & MINUS

- + Needs very little organising, just one person with some tough persuasion skills.
- + No financial outlay.
- + Good result for the time it takes to operate.
- − Just one opportunity, so you need to brief commentators very well.
- − Might find it hard to find the right venue.

BUY A BRICK

... and build a local facility

Operating requirements: Co-ordinator, treasurer.

Equipment needs: Nothing special, just a good filing system.

Lead time: 1 month to set up. A year, or more, to run.

Initial cost: Low level advertising costs.

Suitable for: New buildings, redevelopments or extensions.

Expected return: Several thousand pounds.

What's in it for contributors: Kudos in being listed in the book of sponsors and satisfaction of seeing a project or building take shape which they helped to fund. PR opportunities and advertising in the case of larger company donations.

Frequency: One-off.

Variations on a theme: Buy a theatre seat. Buy a school desk or other equipment.

How does it work?

The idea is to motivate sponsors to contribute to the funding of a building or part of a building. It works especially well where there is already a good feeling of community spirit and where the core population remains fairly static. Village halls, theatres, community centres and sports pavilions are all typical of the kinds of premises that can benefit from this kind of appeal.

Sponsors are invited to pay for a brick at a time – usually £5.00. Their names do not go on each brick but notes are made of all the contributors and a special book listing every donor is drawn up on completion of the building and kept on public display.

For an area that could be tiled internally you might be able to obtain wall tiles that can be decorated by each sponsor or named in their honour. Handmade bricks are probably too expensive to name individually but tiles might not be prohibitive. Alternatively, a good mural can be attractive as well as informative.

HANDY HINT

Start a 'Friends Association' to which every donor automatically becomes a member. After the building is up and running other people can become 'friends' by paying a contribution. 'Friends' benefit from perks, such as special discounts, a week's prior booking for entertainment or entry to special 'Friends Nights'.

How do we get started?

If at all possible divide your project into stages. Perhaps you need an extension to house new kitchens and changing rooms. Plan to raise enough money to build the extension first of all. Then start another appeal for the kitchens and after they are complete go for the changing rooms. People do like to see results and £90,000 just might seem too daunting. Three £30,000 tranches will seem more attainable.

Initially advertise amongst current members or users or, if this is a new venture, to potential users. Send appeal letters, get the press involved to start the appeal and use your community or parish news letters to start the ball rolling. Hold parties or receptions for members or supporters, give talks to groups or organisations, use Rotarian lunches, WI meetings, church groups all to get your message across. Campaign house to house in person if you are really brave, or by leaflet drop if you are short of time or courage. In short, invite absolutely everyone you can think of to 'buy a brick'. Of course they are not really buying a brick as such, but it helps to put the appeal into perspective and they feel good about their contribution being recorded. Make sure all contributors are given a receipt; for large appeals this might be a postcard printed to look like a brick with 'Thank you' engraved on it and some information about the cause, along with a form to make a further contribution, on the back.

Try for commercial donations, perhaps you can persuade a local business to buy a whole wall or fit out the bar or gym. In this case have a plaque professionally prepared and displayed in the appropriate place.

Other generous groups could have rooms named after them or, in the case of a theatre, have a plaque on the back of a seat in the auditorium.

In the case of individuals, you are trading on their vanity; for companies, they will see it as a PR opportunity, so remember to word the invitations accordingly.

PLUS & MINUS

- ⊞ You need no infra-structure, no venue and no cash.
- ⊞ You need very few helpers.
- ⊞ You don't even need to work to a deadline, although the quicker you reach your target, the sooner you can start the first stage.
- ⊟ You do need someone very punctilious to collect the donations and make notes of all the contributors.
- ⊟ You need to keep finding new ways to inject enthusiasm and interest into the project. Momentum can easily die away after the first rush.

Are there any tax advantages?

For tax-paying individuals making a donation of £250 or more to a charity the new Gift Aid scheme can have implications. The charity will be able to claim a repayment of tax and the donor will be able to claim higher rate relief, if appropriate. If you think that you would like to use Gift Aid as a carrot you would be well advised to read the details in the chapter on Tax or study other publications as outlined in the back of the book.

What about when the project is complete?

Throw a party, of course! You can even take the opportunity to make this into another fundraising event with the addition of a raffle or a competition to guess the weight of a pile of bricks. Ask everyone to bring something to eat or drink, persuade someone popular to do the official opening, make a big Thank You speech and hand over the sponsorship book, invite a journalist so that it can be written up for the paper, and start the next appeal with the money that you raised at the party.

Finally, make sure that you keep all the names and addresses of those kind enough to have contributed the first time around, they just might give more for the next stage.

CAROL MARATHON

Sponsored carol singing

Operating requirements: Co-ordinator, treasurer. A choir of volunteer carol singers. Musicians are optional but welcome.

Equipment needs: Collecting tins, several carol books.

Lead time: 6 months.

Initial cost: Nil, unless you need to hire song sheets.

Suitable for: Any charity but particularly good for Christian organisations or schools and church fundraising.

Expected return: Depends largely on where and when your marathon takes place, how big your choir is and how many sponsors they find.

What's in it for contributors: Enjoyment of the Christmas spirit.

Frequency: A one-off at Christmas.

Special requirements: If your event is to take place outside on public land (roads, pavements or a park) you will need to apply for a Street Collection licence.

Variations on a theme: **1.** A sponsored church or school choir sing on their own premises. No collection permit is needed, the space can be warm and comfortable and seats are available for supporters to enjoy the performance. **2.** Same idea, different music; Barbers' Shop to Beatles at all times of the year. **3.** Same idea, different activities; knitting, dancing playing chess etc. **4.** Any of the above played as a competition; the last person still doing the activity is the winner.

How does it work?

Each member of the choir arranges their own sponsorship, perhaps so much per hour or a flat fee if they get to a certain time. The choir sings in a popular area and, in addition to funds raised through sponsorship, a collection tin is regularly handed around the audience.

How do I get started?

Decide on the date and area that you need to sing and apply for a Street Collection Permit from your local authority. You might well have to apply six months, or more, in advance to get the day you want for the busy Christmas period. Contact your chosen charity to borrow some collecting tins and make sure that they are not planning any national collections too near your date. If they are, perhaps you could co-ordinate your appeals. Once you have booked your date you can relax until about a couple of months before.

Organise some sponsorship sheets. Type one up and get it photocopied, it's probably not worth getting them printed unless you have a huge choir and plan a marathon each year.

If you have not already amassed a choir, now is the time. Of course, the bigger the choir, the more sponsors you will get and you may want to take turns, so plan to sign up at least twenty or thirty singers and musicians. Get a firm commitment from each member for the minimum that they will collect and give them a sponsorship form to start using immediately.

When you have your choir complete, hold a meeting and decide how long you are going to aim for. A six – twelve hour marathon really means that you will have to sing in shifts. Three – six hours, and you might make it with the whole choir singing at once, although they are going to be pretty hoarse. You might decide to sing in fancy-dress, it will certainly get you noticed. Perhaps you could devise a novel container for collecting money, say, Santa's boot or a doll's crib.

Start practising as soon as you can, unless you all sing on a regular basis anyway. Vocal chords are like any other parts of the body, use should be increased gradually. You wouldn't dream of playing an hour of squash after you had ' couch-potatoed' for the last twenty years, or if you did, you should not be surprised if the men in white coats came and took you away, that's if you weren't being scraped up by the men in black first!

So, practice at least twice a week and decide a programme. Scores that are tricky to sing should be avoided; you don't want to do yourselves permanent damage.

Plan your route too, unless you are intending to stay in one place, but consider the neighbouring residents and shopkeepers; you don't want to drive them to distraction, think how aggravating buskers become after an hour or two! Remember that December can be pretty chilly so choose places that are not windy and take it in turns to stop and have the occasional sit-down. For a long marathon, arrange a ready supply of thermos flasks of hot coffee and soup. Chocolate bars are a great pick-you-up and milk is thought to be good for the vocal chords, so have supplies on hand.

 **HANDY HINT**

Plan your date to coincide with a late night shopping day so that you can benefit from an extended shopping crowd.

Do we need to advertise?

Not really unless you plan a static performance within a building. A bit of pre-event PR will do no harm at all and you might find your sponsorship forms fill up faster; it's good for the cause too, especially if it is not well known, but you don't need to have posters printed or take an ad in the paper. You are collecting from passers-by, not trying to attract an audience as such. Remember to send a press release out to say how much was raised after the event.

What about afterwards?

If your singers are not too shattered it would be nice to arrange a small party in someone's house or a pub nearby. Organise something hot and easy to eat and drink. Don't expect too much from people, they won't want to stay long, but it is good to extend the feeling of camaraderie a little longer.

Suggest that the singers have two or three weeks to collect their sponsor money and arrange one more meeting to announce your final total and present the cheque to the benefiting charity. Don't forget to thank everyone personally.

PLUS & MINUS

- + No need to hire a venue.
- + Very little organisation.
- + Negligible outlay.
- + Shorter marathon suitable for children over 10.

- − Might find difficulty in recruiting members.
- − Seasonal if using the carol singing idea.

CAR WASH

Car owners pay you to wash their cars

Operating requirements: Co-ordinator, treasurer. Nine helpers, one adult and several children who want to earn some pocket money is ideal.

Equipment needs: Buckets, squeegees and sponges etc. Forget expensive shampoos, washing up liquid is fine. Money apron.

Lead time: 3 weeks.

Initial cost: Say £25 for sponges etc.

Suitable for: Very good for Scout groups but suitable for anything.

Expected return: In a busy car park you could make £250 plus.

What's in it for contributors: A nice shiny car and an opportunity to reappraise their thoughts of 'the youth of today'!

Frequency: Every Saturday. Especially near Christmas.

Special requirements: A reliable and easily available water supply.

Variation on a theme: **1.** House to house washes. **2.** In rural areas, an advertised car wash in the car park of the village hall or local surgery.

How does it work?

There are two ways to work this idea.

Park and Wash: In towns or cities where car parking is at a premium on Saturdays you may be able to find a town centre based company that has it's own car park which is normally used only during the week. Negotiate permission to open the car park to the general public at the weekend and charge for parking (say £3.00) and extra for a car wash (£2.00).

Car Wash only: Here you can ask permission to use NCP or Local Authority car parks. You won't be able to have a slice of the parking fee but you can offer a car wash service to those who park.

How do we get started?

Your hardest problem will be to find a suitable car park to use. You must have a supply of water unless you know a very accommodating farmer or Parks Officer who can leave a full water bowser on site all day.

Many local authorities have a policy of not allowing any sort of trade to operate on their car parks. Councillors may be a little more flexible if they know it is for charity and only a one-off. They could get some

HANDY HINT

Borrow from friends if you can, or commercial cleaning equipment companies might lend you materials or sell them at a discount. Look up Janitorial suppliers in the Yellow Pages.

publicity out of it and if there is one thing politicians cannot refuse, its the promise of some good PR.

A privately owned car park might be a little easier to find, especially if you agree to hand over a percentage of the parking fee. Offer them some publicity too; company directors like the opportunity of being seen in indulgent roles in the local news. Don't forget to erect signs to a private car park. You may have to obtain temporary planning permission for this, although not always if your signs are up for less than twelve hours. Check with your district council.

O.K. so now you have your site sorted out. What about a workforce? Children, 10 years old and upwards, will often be willing and enthusiastic workers, especially before Christmas. Ring round all your friends, put a note up in the school, or speak to youth club leaders, and offer a small wage. You need two people per car and they should be able to wash each one in five to ten minutes, depending on the dirt factor. Make it easy by supplying some decent equipment. You need large buckets, gentle detergent, squeegees (for the windows), big sponges and absorbent, synthetic drying leathers. Really dirty cars will also need a soft hand brush for wheels and in really cold weather it might be kind to offer each helper a pair of rubber gloves. Ideally each team will need one each of all the above, but you might be able to pool resources if your park is not too big. Arrange to meet before you open to the public for some basic training and to ensure that each person knows exactly what is expected of him/her. Plan rest periods to eat or get warm, or cool down. Suggest two hour shifts, or shorter, if you are working with young children.

How do we advertise?

Don't persuade the public to come to you by using costly advertising. You go to them. People going shopping are only concerned about parking their cars as quickly as possible. It is a rare breed who will seek out a new car park especially for the chance to have their car cleaned. By all means advertise with a couple of signs on the car park you plan to use, for a couple of Saturdays prior to your wash day. You could send a press release to your local radio station or newspaper, they might wish to come and take a photo' or two or interview you at the end of the day to see how much you made. Don't bother with leaflets or news ads; it's not worth it.

How do we organise the day?

Display a sign at the entrance explaining that this is a Charity Wash Day and proceeds are going to whatever cause or project. You are more likely to get customers and less likely to risk complaints if people know that you are not a commercial operation.

If you are taking a parking and a wash fee, make sure that an adult is taking money at the entrance. Wear a money apron so that there is less danger of theft and arrange for cash to be collected and taken away regularly. Start with a thirty pound float.

Make sure that all members of the wash team are wearing a brightly coloured waistcoat displaying the charity for whom you are working – you can cut these from thin vinyl, sew on some ties and stick a logo on the front and back. It also adds to visibility and makes the team safer in a busy car park.

Don't bother with parking tickets, just charge a flat fee for the day and adjust the suggested fee to compete with alternative car parks. Shoppers rarely park for more than three hours. Offer the wash at the entrance and if you have an interested customer take for that too. Keep the money separate so that you can tell how many parked and washed or if you have to give a percentage to the owners of the site.

Put something obvious under the windscreen wiper (a square of red paper, for instance) so show the wash team that a car needs washing. As the team get round to washing the waiting cars, they remove the 'flags' and return them to the cashier for re-use.

This system of marking cars is also useful for large public car parks where you are washing only but are particularly busy. It means that your wash team do not have to keep an eye on incoming cars or carry money.

Keep a supply of fluids (for human use!) available and beware of the power of the sun in hot weather. Observe the Australian slogan: Slip, Slap, Slop – slip on a T Shirt, slap on a hat and slop on some sun protection cream.

At the end of the day, clean or mop any areas around the water supply, especially if you have had to go indoors. Rinse out all the equipment and make sure that it goes back to the right owners. Pay the wages and any site fees. Suggest a date when all the children can meet up to find out how much money they made. Give loads of praise and thanks, children (and most adults) need to feel appreciated and you might want to use them again.

PLUS & MINUS

- ⊞ Very little outlay.
- ⊞ Needs little or no advertising.
- ⊞ No need for lengthy organisation.
- ⊞ Great for children over 10.
- ⊞ No sophisticated equipment needed.
- ⊞ Good potential earning power.
- ⊞ Can be used in private or public car parks.
- ⊟ Can be tricky finding a suitable site.
- ⊟ Need at least 8 volunteers plus 1 on the entrance.
- ⊟ Seriously consider Public Liability insurance cover, but you won't be able to insure for damage to cars.

Possible problems?

Charity car washes have had a mixed reception in the past. Owners have had cars damaged, i.e. aerials snapped, paintwork scratched etc. so be aware that not all potential customers will be enthusiastic about the idea.

If you are using children, especially, give a certain amount of training and stress the importance of quality rather than quantity. Try to build a good reputation.

Unfortunately you cannot obtain Public Liability insurance cover for the thing you are working on, i.e. the cars themselves. However if a bucket is left in the way of a pedestrian and he falls over it and breaks a leg you will be covered if he sues. Insurance companies consider that if you are offering a service for payment you should be professional enough to be able to carry it through without causing damage. In any case the car is already insured by the owner, you hope, and companies notoriously dislike insuring anything twice.

If the weather suddenly gets very cold, abandon the idea. A slippery car park is very dangerous and the owners are not going to love you for sloshing water about to provide a skating rink.

COIN PAINTING

Coins are collected to create patterns on the pavement

Operating requirements: Co-ordinator, treasurer. Artist and at least six helpers – possibly children.

Equipment needs: Washable paints, chalks or huge area of blank newsprint. Cones and ropes.

Lead time: 2 months.

Initial cost: Less than £30.

Suitable for: All types of charities. Needs to take place in a safe pedestrian area, a security protected shopping mall is ideal.

Expected return: Over £100, possibly considerably more.

What's in it for contributors: An opportunity to take part in a unique and transient piece of art.

Frequency: One-off.

Special requirements: You need a reliable venue, this idea is particularly vulnerable to theft and vandalism.

Variations on a theme: Draw the outline of a giant dinosaur in the playground, children cover the lines with 2 pence pieces.

How does it work?

An artist paints a reasonably simple design onto the ground. Passers-by are encouraged to place a coin in the appropriate place for its denomination to build up the picture. The picture is 'painted' until it is finished or for the whole shopping day, whichever is the shortest. It is unrealistic to try to go beyond about 5.30pm. At the end, photographs are taken for posterity and all the coins swept up and taken to the bank to convert into a cheque for the benefiting charity.

HANDY HINT

Contact your regional Arts Board to explain your project, they just might be able to think of an artist who would be prepared to help you.

How do I get started?

First find your artist – someone well known adds to the news-worthiness of the event. In the absence of a home-grown Jasper Johns, try offering the idea to the local Art School; tutors might like to run a project and choose the best design.

Whilst finding your designer, look for a suitable venue. It may be that your area doesn't have a Mall or an Arndale Centre to offer. You could use a large floor space in a sports hall or a cathedral but I feel you really need a continuous stream of people walking by to make this idea work well. Consider the possibility of a pedestrian precinct or a well used park in the Summer, but you must be reasonably sure that your helpers are not going to get mugged or the whole design mown down by vandals on cycles.

Explain that you will be using temporary paints or chalks that can be washed off easily. If you agree a venue in principle, but the owners cannot be convinced about the materials, you will have to lower your sights a little to beg a quantity of newsprint from a local newspaper. Failing this you will just have to get out the lining paper and some glue! Or...you could stick the outlines of the design onto the ground using coloured tapes ... but make sure that what ever you do, it is BIG.

If you have a large space to fill, consider just drawing outlines. Coins of all denominations can be placed all along the lines to create the design. For a smaller space solid colours should be used and the coins placed over each colour to build up individual blocks. This is explained in more detail further on in this chapter.

Do we need to advertise?

Well maybe not using leaflets or posters. I would go for something a little more subtle. Suppose you have a student at the local Art School geared up to be your creative input and you have an agreement to 'paint' your coin picture in the local shopping mall which just happens to be owned by a large insurance company.

If you were the director of that company could you see some good PR mileage in making a picture based on the theme of your company's work or, more prosaically, the company's corporate symbol? Too right you could! It's manna from heaven and you'd be a fool not to grab the idea and milk it for all it's worth.

Having got the company PR department interested, all you may have to do is be available while they organise media releases. If you have a famous artist involved you could even get TV coverage. On the other hand, it could be part of the bargain that you do the running around.

Some companies might even be prepared to meet, pound for pound, the amount raised, providing a form of sponsorship.

Finally, whilst not strictly advertising, you need to warn the surrounding businesses a week or so in advance so that they can prepare themselves with additional quantities of small change as people will want to change notes so that they can be take part.

How do we organise the day?

On the Saturday prior, display some signs explaining the event for the following week.

On the morning of the day, pace out the area that you will need and surround it with cones (or stools) and ropes to keep the space clear. Lay down a few caps or hats so that people can contribute as the artist is preparing the ground.

At this stage she/he is operating rather like a pavement artist. The

PLUS & MINUS

- ⊞ Very little outlay.
- ⊞ No need for a committee.
- ⊞ Children can be involved.
- ⊞ High profile event.
- ⊞ Attracts many contributors

- ⊟ Coins will almost all be small denominations.
- ⊟ Big commitment to find the right venue and artist, probably needs good negotiating skills.
- ⊟ Need several helpers, especially if you have to scrub the area clean at the end.

work should be built up using just three colours (large areas will be in just two colours) to coincide with the brass, copper and silver colours of our coinage. As she/he completes one area you can invite the public to start to fill in the space with coins. Use the money collected in the hats to start off a patch. Hopefully the artist will have used one colour to paint small but very important parts of the picture, such as eyes or jewellery. These areas should be reserved for pound coins; there will be some people who would only contribute 10p in the normal course of events, but faced with the opportunity to 'paint' a mouth or other unique part of the picture, will happily contribute several pound coins just so they can say 'I did that'.

If a crowd develops, or as the picture gets bigger, you will want to prevent people stamping about over the area. Now your helpers come into play. Keep the barriers up and use your boy scouts, or whoever, to place the coins for people. Put your helpers in uniform or coloured waistcoats marked with the charity logo or ask them to wear all the same colours. It helps contributors find someone to give their money to quickly and easily.

As the picture draws to completion, contact the local radio station and newspaper office and give your local TV newsroom a ring to say that you will be finished in about an hour. Work out a very rough estimate of how much the picture is 'worth'.

Arrange for a professional photographer to take some pictures at the end and suggest that the Mayor or company chairman might like to be photographed placing a final rosette of fivers to make the finishing touch.

Be ready with your brooms to sweep everything up and don't forget plenty of buckets or money bags to carry your spoils away; coins are incredibly heavy.

You may be able to leave the painted design on the ground until it wears off but you must be prepared to wash and scrub it all off there and then, if required.

Possible problems?

Paint looks much more striking than chalk but some paints wash off some surfaces better than others. Take advice from a commercial paint company (they may even supply the paint free of charge). Try a small area first and prove to your, and the owners of the venue's satisfaction that it will come off easily. Chalk may take a few showers to completely disappear but some scrubbing brushes should do the trick fairly quickly.

EVENT 8

CREAM TEAS

Home-made teas for sale in the garden

Operating requirements: Co-ordinator, treasurer and helpers.

Equipment needs: Trestle tables, picnic tables and chairs, insulated cool boxes, crockery and cutlery, hot water urn, electrical supply and a couple of catering sized tea pots.

Lead time: 4-6 weeks.

Initial cost: Under £25 for advertising, plus costs of ingredients

Suitable for: Local fundraising. Churches, village halls, hospices etc.

Expected return: As in the barbecue, aim to make three or four times your ingredients costs. If scones and cakes are donated, so much the better.

What's in it for contributors: An event particularly suited to retired and elderly people although it by no means excludes families. A taste of yesteryear Britain.

Frequency: Two, or at the most three, times during the Summer at different venues.

How does it work?

There are three ways to operate your Cream Tea.

1. Cream Teas are offered to passing trade in much the same way that you might expect a Tea Garden to work in the West Country, the difference being that this event relies on publicity to bring people in on a one-off occasion. You will need sign-posting and advertising to make this work well.

2. You can sell tickets to the general public. This gives you a good opportunity to judge the quantities of provisions needed and puts money in the kitty before you open. (See the chapter on Barbecues.) Again you will need a good advertising campaign, although, because you have a longer period of time in which to sell your tickets, word-of-mouth will be a valuable asset.

3. You can sell tickets through invitation only. If you have a small town garden or appeal to a very small potential customer base fundraising for a very specialised organisation, you might find this is the option for you especially if you invite a celebrity or several VIPs. Everyone can do something and you are really holding a private party for which you ask a small contribution. But you are not going to make pots of gold.

I favour variation 1 unless you are forced into option 3, because firstly, in variation 2 you have the additional expense of the tickets themselves and secondly, when confronted by plates full of goodies you may well find that your customers will be tempted to buy more than they had intended, which will enhance your profits.

Charging £2.00 or so for a ticket may seem quite expensive for a cup of tea, a scone with cream and jam and a piece of cake and you might put some people off. However, the individual cost of two delicious scones, oozing strawberries and cream, a slice of chocolate cake and a flapjack washed down by a couple of cups of tea, all mounts up. Just think of all those calories! Perhaps you should sell diet sheets on the way out!

How do we get started?

First decide on your venue (probably a nice garden but don't rule out an accessible river bank, a pretty barn or even a church yard or hall if you are in an urban environment) and a date that does not coincide with any other local summer activity. You should also decide for whom you are planning your Cream Tea. The people who really enjoy this type of event are the older age groups, so make it their event with tranquil surroundings, chairs to sit on and china cups to drink from; although you need to make sure that you have a supply of squash and biscuits for children.

Confirm a supply of chairs and folding tables. A couple of trestle tables covered with clean sheets or cloths are useful also. Don't forget to book your supply of crockery and some spoons and knives well in advance. You may be able to hire these from a village or church hall or a community centre. The same source might be able to supply an urn and some tea pots although many commercial catering suppliers, such as Looses in East Anglia have everything for hire, even for quite small quantities.

Advertise your event in local shops, at the over 60s club, the doctor's and dentist's surgeries, libraries, in the local paper or anywhere where retired people, in particular, visit.

If the garden where you are holding your event is very special, you might consider asking a nominal entrance charge. It all helps to swell the funds. You might also think about holding a croquet tournament at the same time. This is often extremely popular and some players are very competitive and might bring a number of spectators.

By now you will have a good idea how many people are likely to come and you will have to work out how much food you need. Buy some catering packs of good quality tea, sugar and strawberry jam. It will always keep if you don't use it all. Ask volunteers to make scones, cakes and biscuits or order them from the local baker, although your profits will dwindle quickly if you have to buy your goods. If you have some left over you can freeze them or sell them off at the end. Or you could hold a raffle for all the leftovers. Reckon on getting nine slices out of an average sized cake. Buy whipping cream on the morning of the event, but order it from the dairy first to be sure of having enough. If you live in the South West, you might choose to use clotted cream instead. Have plenty of butter available in case people don't like cream or if you run out.

HANDY HINT

To get nine slices from a round cake: first cut out a very slightly smaller than usual slice by eye and remove it. Cut the cake in half from the centre of the cake out to the edge exactly opposite the middle of the missing slice. Now shift one half round slightly so that you have two thin slices missing on either side. Cut the cake in half again to form four large triangles which you half again into eight slices. With the slice you first removed you now have nine slices from an eight slice cake! Sneaky? Who, me?

How do we run the day?

If you are charging an entrance fee, station your collector near the gate a good ten minutes before you officially open. Make sure they have a chair and someone to relieve them after an hour or so. It helps to have a sign up showing the logo and name of your charity and what is going on. Fly some bunting if you have some, it all adds a bit of atmosphere.

Arrange an area for people to park their cars safely although most people will come on foot.

Keep your serving tables all together, probably near an electric socket for your urn and preferably in the shade. Ensure that all trailing flexes are covered with mats or, ideally, string them up at least seven feet above the ground. Wrap plugs and electric sockets in plastic bags in case of sudden downpours. Keep your route to the house away from the flexes.

If you have enough helpers, keep one person to collecting money only. It is not very hygienic to be handling money and food.

Although tea, cakes and biscuits are not very high risk foods, fresh cream is, so to be on the safe side keep only small quantities of cream and cream-filled cakes or scones on the table. Use cool boxes or the fridge in the house, if it is not too far away, to store supplies until they are needed.

ANOTHER HANDY HINT

Fill cakes with fresh cream and jam, or fresh fruit, only as you use them. Any left over will not be wasted and can be frozen safely. You can freeze cream to use for cooking also. Pour it into ice-cube containers so that you can defrost small amounts at a time.

How can we maximise profits?

You might need to do something more than just sell teas to make your efforts worthwhile. Don't be tempted to add too much in the way of entertainment; in my experience the most memorable events, however humble, are those that have a special identity and don't just seem like the ubiquitous fete.

Make more cakes than are needed to raffle at the end or just sell whole for freezing. (Don't fill these with jam or cream. Butter icing is ideal.)

Have a 'Guess the weight of the cake' competition. (See the chapter on Stalls and Sideshows.)

Hold a raffle for an appropriate donated prize.

You could have a plant stall or garden produce stand, especially if you know your visitors are keen gardeners.

PLUS & MINUS

- + Not difficult to organise.
- + No expensive venue to hire.
- + Small capital outlay.
- + Not very labour intensive on the day.

- − You do need to mobilise lots of volunteers to bake the goodies.
- − Not a great money spinner.
- − Limited appeal, but absolutely right for some areas.

EVENT 9

CUSTOMISED SCHOOLKIT AND CABOODLE

School items for sale designed by the students

Operating requirements: Co-ordinator (member of the school staff), treasurer, sales people.

Equipment needs: Customised produce as detailed below. Stall, or semi-permanent base within school.

Lead time: 3 to 4 months.

Initial cost: Entirely dependent on the amount of stock you order. Usually payment not required until 30 days after receipt of goods so take payment with orders so that you can be sure of paying the bills.

Suitable for: Schools, large play groups or nurseries, special needs centres.

Expected return: Usually you charge two or three times what it costs to buy.

What's in it for purchasers: Seeing their children's drawings in print – the 'Ahh Goo' factor! Good quality useful items, professionally produced.

Frequency: Continuous.

Special requirements: Needs to be run like a business, with accounts and possibly VAT.

Variations on a theme: Home designed Christmas cards (not to be confused with selling charity cards) and other stationery.

How does it work?

Children prepare drawings of themselves, their chums or their school. The drawings are professionally printed onto various items – tea towels, kit bags, shoe bags, laundry bags, peg bags, T shirts, notelets, table mats etc. These are sold for profit. You could have a stall at the school fete or, at larger schools, there may be a semi-permanent 'shop' available.

HANDY HINT

Give children frames or squares of paper so that they all produce drawings roughly the same size. You can use signatures but 'portraits' are far more appealing.

How do we get started?

Find a printer who is prepared to print from your designs. Make sure that the quality of products is good enough; some T shirts are very cheap but poorly made.

I do not usually want to advertise specific companies but, in my opinion, Countryside Art in Lincolnshire are second to none in providing this service. (Address at the back of the book.) They are used to working with schools from all over the country and provide clear instructions and template sizes to achieve just what you want. The quality and variety of goods is excellent.

Contact your printers at least three months in advance (more if you need things before Christmas) and find out what lead time they need to print your items from the time they receive your finished art work.

To make the whole idea a little special you can arrange a project for members of the whole school or group to each produce a drawing on white paper using a new black felt-tipped pen.

Make sure that you see a sample before printing the whole run, or at least visit the works to agree the art work.

Its a good idea to bag all the goods up individually which helps to keep everything clean as well as looking professional, some companies will do this automatically. When you receive your items you will have to price them and decide how to sell them if you haven't already done so.

Market your stall or shop, prior to opening, with A5 leaflets showing a price list and where the goods are available. Give a phone number or contact name so that people can discuss orders that they may wish to collect on a specific day. You could even take orders before you go ahead with the printing, although the products are so attractive they usually sell better where customers can see them. Remember that there will be a minimum order.

Possible problems?

Make sure that your organisation is registered as a charity if possible as this will give you certain grant and tax advantages. See the back of the book for details about VAT and for relevant publications.

PLUS & MINUS

- + Potential for making large profit.
- + No special venue required.
- + Initial drawing project involves children of any age and could be run as a special event in itself.
- + Very attractive products that every member of the family and friends will be queuing to buy.
- + Companies specialised in this service already set up.
- + Few helpers needed.

- − Need school's co-operation and site for shop if 'going permanent'.
- − Has to be run as a business. May involve large quantities of cash. Possible VAT registration. Charity status and bank account advantageous.

EVENT 10

DUTCH AUCTION

All the thrill of an auction without the expense.

Operating requirements: Auctioneer and/or co- ordinator, treasurer, collector, two or more stewards.

Equipment needs: Venue preferably with a stage, if not you will need a podium of some sort. Chairs for the audience and room to display items to be auctioned. Collecting box or plate. Timer.

Lead time: A month to six weeks to set up the event but you might need several months to collect all the items.

Initial cost: Usually a dutch auction takes place as part of another event; perhaps a dinner, wine and cheese party or maybe an art exhibition and will cost very little to stage. If you have managed to collate some really splendid items to be auctioned you should hold the event in its own right, print catalogues, market it well and attract a really large audience. This could cost you £50 – £100.

Suitable for: Particularly good for local causes when used as an added attraction to something else. When holding a Dutch Auction as the main event it will need to be for a popular, current or nationally known cause.

Expected return: Your return will depend largely on the size of your audience as well as the quality and popularity of the goods offered. For a large event you could make £1,000 or more.

What's in it for contributors: The opportunity to buy something for considerably less than its real value and to experience the excitement and thrill of a real auction with none of the risk.

Frequency: Annual.

Special requirements: It helps if you produce a celebrity auctioneer.

How does it work?

Variation 1: The auctioneer offers items for sale as in a conventional auction. At the first bid s/he will start the timer which is kept secret from the audience. The first bid will come in at, perhaps, £1.00 A steward will collect the pound from the bidder in a collection box. The next bid may be £1.50 and the steward will collect 50p; this being the balance to make up the £1.50 in the box. The next bidder might bid £2.25 but will only have to pay 75p and so on. The bidding continues until the timer rings and stops the bidding. The person making the last bid has the goods.

You could arrange for the steward to just make a record of names and amounts, if everyone is known to the stewards or auctioneer, payment can then be made in a lump sum at the end of the evening.

Variation 2: The auctioneer opens the bidding himself and lowers it in stages until a buyer is found. I feel some of the excitement is lost using this variation as you are not bidding against anyone else. However, there is an element of anticipation in case you lose a coveted item to someone else.

If you print catalogues before the event they can be sold to use as tickets or numbered, to hold a raffle, or sell advertising space to raise more funds.

You can run a Dutch Auction with just one or two really special items for sale, such as a holiday or a television, and, if you are using Variation 1, it is the auctioneer's responsibility to see that he gets at least one bid from everyone in the room. The timer should be set to allow one bid every 20 seconds, to allow the stewards to collect the money, or three bids a minute. Multiply the time by the number of guests, give or take a minute or two, and you should be able to run up some serious bidding. At this type of event most contenders will up the bidding by at least £5.00, so with 100 guests you might expect to make £500 in just over 30 minutes.

If you have plenty of smaller goods people will raise the biding by pence rather than pounds but everyone will have fun bidding several times for lots of different goods. Add a few surprises in kind such as for the promise auction (a couple of hours gardening or an offer to cook a meal). It is surprising how much can be made on really popular items so judge the timing appropriately. Put a couple of really short times in – sort of loss leaders – to inject some excitement whenever you feel interest is flagging.

How do I get started?

You might need to get together a small committee and delegate special duties. It can be very time consuming collecting goods for sale or finding someone prepared to be auctioneer. You may have to store goods for sometime also so you need to consider somewhere secure. Obtain a logo from your benefiting charity for use on publicity.

First you need to collect your sale goods. For special prizes try non-chain stores for donations and some holiday companies are prepared to help so long as you can guarantee good PR and publicity; which is where your VIP comes in.

If you know an artist or sculptor who is particularly sympathetic to your cause you could ask if they would be prepared to offer an original piece of work to be auctioned.

The celebrity personality and the prizes are a bit of a chicken and egg situation. The VIP might be more prepared to help out if s/he feels that you have some big 'prizes' to offer and the stores are more prepared to make donations if they know you have a big name to add weight to potential media interest.

For smaller auctions you will have to ask for donations locally. If people can't find something in their attics that will do, ask them to bake a cake, give some vegetables or plants or make something special. Get a specific commitment out of people if you can without being pushy. The local pub, shop or restaurant might give a free meal or a voucher.

Next, decide on a date and venue, or if your auction is to be part of a larger event, and check that it is convenient for your auctioneer.

Now you have to work out how you are to market the event. You have two choices. Either you advertise as you would for a theatrical show or you send invitations. If you advertise to the general public it is probably helpful to sell tickets in advance. The hall you hire will hold a fire certificate which dictates how large your audience is. It would be very sad to have to turn away people on the night if your auction was very popular and it could be tempting to sell more tickets than you should.

Don't forget to involve all the media. Send press releases to newspapers, radio, even television if your celebrity is a really big name. Advertise carefully or give due consideration to your guest list.

Tickets can be free or paid for but you do need them, if only to work out how many people are coming. If they are paid for, you could use the entrance money to buy the sale goods if you are not successful with donations, or to hire a stage personality from an agency.

Lastly you need to ensure that there is enough car parking for your patrons. If you expect a really large crowd in a small village or a part of town that does not provide enough parking it is a courtesy to inform the police. They will be happy to advise you and might wish to control the area.

What happens on the big day?

Set the hall out like a theatre, i.e. chairs all facing a stage area. Provide a separate room for viewing the goods if necessary or place them round the auditorium. They need to marked with lot numbers.

After the main attraction (in the event of a dinner people remain seated where they are) or at the appointed hour, the auctioneer starts the bidding in the manner described above. S/he will work from a numbered sheet and ask stewards to bring the lots forward or pass them along the rows for people to examine where appropriate. In the event of a few very special lots this will not be necessary.

The more charismatic and persuasive your auctioneer is, and if you have chosen someone local it helps if they know most of the people present, the more bids you are likely to get.

Most people will come to the auction planning to spend a fixed amount and towards the end more and more people will sit out of the bidding because they have reached their ceiling. Of course you want to make as much money from the event as you can, but it is unfair to shame people into spending more than they wish. To keep everyone interested and to let the auction end on a high note save the best lot until last but let it be known from the start that this is planned. You don't want to be left in a situation where bidders are 'all spent out' and you have very few bids for your star item. Everyone can join in one more time and after it is all over they know it is time to go home.

Is there anything we should do afterwards?

Thank everyone profusely for supporting the event and arrange for a bouquet or something special to thank your auctioneer (to be presented in front of the audience). Make sure that you have planned for some help in tidying up and if it is very late, leave it until the morning if possible.

It will always be appreciated if you write a letter of thanks for all large donations and include the final figure for your proceeds. Write an official letter of thanks to your auctioneer as it is a very stressful job. People do like to know how things turned out and they will be more willing to contribute or attend again if they feel you were grateful and the event was a success. Send another of the ubiquitous news releases saying how brilliant the auction was, how many people came and include a quotation from your auctioneer if possible. Tag on a date and invitation to attend an official paying over of the money raised to the charity.

Possible problems?

It just might be that people are not sure what happens at a Dutch Auction. If you begin to sense that people are in the dark as to what is expected of them, prepare an A5 photocopied sheet of 'How it works' to send or give to those who ask. If you are organising Variation 1 as a small local affair without invitations, add a line saying something like, 'bring plenty of small change' or 'all cash bids under 50p', to all the posters.

PLUS & MINUS

- ⊞ Can piggyback another event.
- ⊞ You can raise funds from entrance tickets, the sale of advertising space in catalogues and the auction itself.
- ⊞ Needs little in the way of special equipment.
- ⊞ Flexible. Could be all over in 20 minutes or take a couple of hours.
- ⊟ Can be time consuming in the organising.
- ⊟ Audience might need explanation of what is expected of them.
- ⊟ Not suitable for children.

FAST PARTY

People pay not to attend a dinner

Operating requirements: Just two people can organise this non-event! Actually one could do the work but, as with all fundraising, it is as well to have two heads checking money.

Equipment needs: Some really beautifully designed invitations and someone with a witty brain.

Lead time: A couple of weeks.

Initial cost: Just the cost of the invitations (unless you can get a friendly printer to sponsor the event for a little advertising on the reverse of each invite). And postage.

Suitable for: Well known organisations, either local or national. Especially good for aid charities; if the event is taken seriously it can show a solidarity with victims.

Expected return: Well the sky's the limit. Keep your 'tickets' to about £2.50 per couple or family and you will find it surprisingly successful. This idea works best if you send invitations to people you know personally so if you combine your efforts with a couple of others you can widen your guest list.

What's in it for contributors: First, they don't have to respond at all if they don't like the idea. Second, lots of people like to support a particular group but they often don't like an 'organised' social event; they may have small children, not have a car or are elderly and not be able to get out much; they may not be able to afford £10–£15 for a special dinner. A Fast Party allows them to show support at a relatively low cost without having to give up valuable time and effort. And no one can be 'busy on the night'!

Frequency: A 'one-off' event. It might be better to restrict your use of this idea; it is amusing and clever once but some people might feel it is a bit of a con if you use it too often.

What is a Fast Party?

It is not a party held in double-quick time! No, 'fast' is as in not eating. Sounds pretty strange. How does it work?

Guests are invited to a party that will not take place. They are asked to go without one meal on a particular date and to contribute the cost of that meal to the proceeds. They may or may not take part in the spirit of the event, but many are happy to contribute anyway.

HANDY HINT

This idea could work well as a form of PR. Make sure that you prepare a couple of good Press Releases, before and after, for your local newspapers, radio stations and charity newsletters.

What's my starting point?

Find two or three other people to help write a guest list and pool some ideas for a witty invitation. Work on the premise that 'guests' might like the chance to show off a very flashy invitation on their mantelpieces, even if it is for a bit of a laugh. Something like this might do, but I'm sure you can think of something better:

Have the invitations printed on a good quality card and of a standard size to fit into an envelope and include a self-addressed envelope to encourage the cheques to roll in. (The printer will probably supply envelopes cheaper than at a retail stationers.) If you think you might repeat the 'event' annually, you can have extra printed at very little extra cost. Remember to leave the date line clear so that you can write in the new date next year.

MR AND MRS ......

(Your name or organisation)

have pleasure in not requesting your presence at a

FAST PARTY

in aid of

BARKSWORTH DOGS HOME

not to be held on Saturday 20th June

not at Growlnsnap Grange

The guests of honour will not include

HER MAJESTY THE QUEEN'S CORGI

THE LORD MAYOR OF BARKSWORTH

RSVP
(address.......)

Tickets in advance
£2.50 per couple
(Cheques payable to......)

Guests are invited to give up one meal for this worthy cause and donate the cost to the above address.

What if I get very few replies?

You should get at least 50% donating something. If you think you should have done better you could try a follow up call and offer to pop round to collect, without being pushy. Some people may not wish to contribute for whatever reason and you should respect their decision but others may have just forgotten and welcome a call to save them going to the post box.

Should I do anything after the date is past?

Well, apart from handing the proceeds over, it is a nice idea to send a short thank you letter. This could be photocopied to keep costs down – keep a note of any specially generous donations so that you reply personally. To add to the theme you could print a revolting menu on the back to show what they would be thankful to have missed! Remember to add the cost of the thank-yous and the postage to your budget.

Any problems?

It may be better to have cheques made out to the charity itself as personal cheques are easy to abuse. Contributors may be happier writing cheques direct to a cause that they know and trust. Check with your benefiting group as to how they would like to receive the money.

PLUS & MINUS

- + Very little organising necessary
- + No venue, no nothing!
- + Surprisingly effective
- + Very little outlay
- + Fairly easy to obtain sponsorship
- − Limited use
- − Best used on friends and family who might feel a bit used or under obligation. Try to give them a good laugh for their money

EVENT 12

GARDEN OPEN DAY

Open your garden to the public for an entrance fee

Operating requirements: Garden owners prepared to have hordes of nosy people tramping over their property. One or two organisers. Stall holders and refreshments stall holders if required.

Equipment needs: Table and chair for entrance fee collector. Tables for stalls, tea and buns paraphernalia (see Cream Teas) if required. Signs.

Lead time: Two or three months, or longer if a series is arranged, to allow for advertising.

Initial cost: £25

Suitable for: Just about anything. The beauty of this idea is that it is infinitely flexible. For a WI fundraiser add a splendid tea tent and produce stalls. For a Mums and Tots group add a Teddy Bear's Picnic and a supervised paddling pool. For the Gardening Club add plant stalls. For the school add a treasure hunt or quiz stalls; the list is endless.

Expected return: This might depend on the weather and the amount of additional attractions. Charge 50p/£1.00 entry, children under 10 free and nearly all your takings will be profit.

What's in it for visitors: An undemanding few hours out and an opportunity to catch up with a few friends. For the keen gardener it can be a time to get some ideas or buy some new specimens. For others...well, never underestimate the curiosity of folk. If the local 'big hoos' – as they say in Scotland – can be persuaded to open its gates, doors, swimming pool, tennis court etc: you might be amazed at how many people will come just to be nosy!

Frequency: This idea is perfect for a summer series of open gardens all in the area or it can be just as effective as a one-off. It is perhaps best not to open the same garden more than twice a year.

Special requirements: If you are serious about making this a real gardening day then a couple of knowledgeable horticulturists on hand to answer questions is a must.

How does a Garden Open Day work?

Very simply, you are charging an entry fee for people to see around someone's private garden. You will need to make sure that there is not another entrance where visitors can get in without paying. It is unlikely that you will get gate-crashers at this type of event but visitors do make genuine mistakes. You may or may not have added attractions to supplement the entrance money.

How do I get started?

Form a little group of organisers, it need only be two, decide on a garden and persuade the owner that they won't mind their private space invaded.

Contact the group for whom you are fundraising to make sure that they are happy for you to use this idea and are not in competition with another of their events. Then check with the local Tourist Information Centre and Central Library that you are not opening on the same day as another garden in the same area.

You may have other objectives than just raising money. If so, work out what else you wish to achieve, i.e. giving the patients from a local hospice a day out, or teaching teenagers about looking after the countryside. Whatever it is make sure that you theme your additional activities to your objective or to the flavour of your benefiting group.

HANDY HINT

Ask the owners of the garden to present prizes, join the panel of 'experts' or be involved in some way. It helps them to feel part of the day and prevents the impression that your organisation has in some way 'taken over'.

What if I own a lovely garden and want to open it in a good cause, but don't quite know what?

There are at least three organisations that run Garden Open Days throughout the country: the Red Cross, St. John Ambulance and the National Garden Scheme. The address of the headquarters of the latter can be found at the back of the book and you will find the regional headquarters for the two first aid organisations listed in your local yellow pages.

How do I publicise my event?

Decide if you want your garden day to be a strictly local affair or if you would like visitors from all over. Of course if the garden is only small or you are fundraising for a very local charity it would be better to restrict your publicity to the surrounding area.

Always adjust a general approach to your particular needs. Remember, the further afield your audience is, the more advertising time you need to allow.

Advertise in local garden centres, you might be able to persuade a journalist to interview you for the gardening section in the local paper or on local radio. Advertise in the charity's newsletter or at other events. How about organising a gardening quiz for the local paper with the winner becoming the VIP to open the Garden Day? Or meeting the 'personality' booked to open the event.

Don't waste money having huge A1 posters screen printed. A4 or at the most A3 posters are all you need. Just black on a colour or outlines on white paper that children can colour in are effective. You might find A5 leaflets are all that is needed. You can photocopy a few large sizes for shops or notice boards.

Distribution is everything. Place them where they are most effective. Try getting an insert service with the community newsletter or parish magazine. See if you can obtain a list of gardening club members and deliver leaflets direct or advertise at one of their shows. Members of local heritage and conservation groups may also be interested.

For larger events, use the Tourist Information listings and the 'What's On' features in all the local media. Teletext and Oracle will list local attractions also.

Always make it clear for whom you are fundraising. Remember, date and time, place, what the event comprises, a contact name and telephone number and the price.

What do I do about parking cars?

If your event attracts people from out of the immediate area you will have to think about where to park cars. The ideal is a field or a long drive but there are not many places that can provide this. If you are relying on cars parked on the road it might be a good idea to contact the police and hear their suggestions. They might want to put a line of cones in sensitive areas. Don't forget to signpost the car park.

You could charge for car parking, but in my experience, for a gentle event like this, you would be best advised to cut your losses and let the parking look after itself free of charge. You probably don't want two or three people tied up all day collecting money and parking cars.

If the weather has been wet or the grass is rather long you may find a well used path from the car park to the entrance gate becoming slippery and dangerous. Preclude any accidents by pegging down wire netting securely over any problem areas. It helps stop people sliding and it protects the grass underneath.

What else can I have in the garden?

This rather depends on the space you have available but try to keep activities limited or to a strictly gardening theme or you might as well be holding a fete.

The following are just a few ideas that you might include:

- A leaf or flower quiz: leaves or flowers from the garden are stuck onto a board and numbered. Contestants pay to enter and are given a sheet of paper on which they write their names and telephone number and list the numbers with the corresponding names of the trees or plants from which they think the leaves or flowers have come. The winner is the first correct list drawn at a certain time or at the end of the day. A prize should be donated.
- Garden produce stall
- Home made produce stall
- Plant stall
- Wicker work, corn dollies or dried flower stall
- Treasure hunt: contestants pay to enter and are given a list of items to find. They can either look for numbers stuck on the objects (to prevent damage or removal) or write down where they have seen them. The winner is the first correct entry drawn as before.
- Teas or barbecue: see separate chapters.
- If the garden has a swimming pool, tennis court, croquet lawn or other facilities make a charge to use them.
- Have some music and make a charge for requests.

- Garden Answers stand: Customers are invited to bring specimens from their own gardens or ask questions for help from an expert or experts. Make a small charge for each answer.
- Blade sharpening stand
- Second hand or reconditioned gardening tools stand
- Raffle for a donated piece of garden equipment or perhaps a painting of a countryside scene. Remember raffles have to be drawn before the end of the day if you want to avoid being registered for a lotteries licence.

PLUS & MINUS

- \+ Venue is free.
- \+ Very flexible, making the idea suitable for all groups.
- \+ Family event.
- \+ Can use on-site facilities as added attractions.
- \+ Can operate with very few organisers but you might need more if you have a lot of additional activities.
- − Relies on the weather.
- − Needs to be fenced, but most gardens are.
- − Needs arrangements for car parking.

EVENT 13

HOST-A-SALE

Shopping at home

Operating requirements: One host.

Equipment needs: Nothing other than you will have available at home.

Lead time: 2 or 3 months.

Initial cost: Nil, unless you send invitations by post and provide a few refreshments, in which case you will have the cost of the stamps and tea and biscuits.

Suitable for: Making a donation to any charity. Particularly good for women (probably) at home during the day or evening.

Expected return: Unlikely to be more than £20 or £30. If you use a public hall you could earn substantially more.

What's in it for contributors: Opportunity for a bit of a get together and to buy things without having to visit the shops.

Frequency: Best kept to a couple of times a year.

Special requirements: Suitable party plan company.

How does it work?

This is how Tupperware started in the US. A representative of the company comes to your house to demonstrate or display items for sale to a group of invited friends. It is usual to offer refreshments and a party atmosphere.

The rep will bring a set of display items and takes orders to be delivered to you to distribute. Payment to you, for the use of your home and friends, is a percentage of the value of the orders taken in goods or cash.

You may be able to persuade the company to give you cash, but if they insist on goods you can then hold a raffle on another day when you invite everyone back to collect their goods to save you the cost of distribution.

That seems a lot of work for a pretty small return, I hear you say. Well, maybe, but if you can offer the company a large potential market (i.e. you ask 20 – 25 friends) or a group of you club together and hire a room in the local community centre at an off-peak time and pool an invitation list so that you can expect 50 – 100 people, you will be more successful in bartering for cash, especially if you explain the cause.

How much organising is there?

It really won't be much work, I promise you, and you should have some fun. The company supply all the invitations and all you have to do is fill them in and give them to your friends. The representative will arrive about half an hour before you start and if you clear a table for her use she will do everything else.

If you plan to hold your party during the day and you invite young mums or dads, make sure that you allocate a play space for preschool children and delegate someone to look after the 'creche' if you invite a good crowd. Make it clear to people that there is no obligation to buy.

If you are worried about the amount of distribution work you will have after the party, ensure that you only invite people that you see regularly or who you see in a group, such as when you collect your children at school.

PLUS & MINUS

- ⊞ Needs very little organising.
- ⊞ You can hold the party in your own home.
- ⊞ No need for other helpers.
- ⊟ Probably not going to make much more than a token donation, but its a good excuse to have some friends over.
- ⊟ The party plan company might insist on you being paid in goods.

So who are all these Party Plan companies?

Of course there is Tupperware itself and you will find your local distributors, from whom you can book a demonstrator, listed in Yellow Pages under Party Planners; Red House Books, a children's and educational publications book club – The Red House, Witney, Oxford OX8 5YF; Robert Norfolk, women's and children's clothes but specialising in designer sweat shirts – Dualford Ltd, 67 Gatwick Road, Crawley, Sussex RH10 2RD, Colour me Beautiful – home colour consultants – 56 Abbey Business Centre, Ingate Place, London SW8 3NS, to name but four.

There are also numerous local companies, usually 'cottage industries' manufacturing clothes, jewellery, cosmetics or furniture. Try putting an enquiry advertisement in your local paper and see what you come up with. Local and privately owned companies are more likely to bend company policy to give you what you want. Companies like Tupperware might be helpful but you will probably have to wait for comments to arrive from head office.

100 CLUB

One hundred people contribute to a fundraising club

Operating requirements: A minimum of 2; Promoter and Treasurer. Additional invited monthly assistance in drawing the numbers. It helps if 10 contributors agree to be responsible for collections.

Equipment needs: Box of 100 small cubes (usually wooden) each numbered clearly 1 to 100.

Lead time: 2-3 months

Initial cost: £50 setting up fee (£35 initial registration with your Local Authority and basic advertising costs). £17.50 annual renewal fee.

Suitable for: Small-time, on-going fundraising where there is a reasonably static population and a perennial need to raise small amounts of money for maintenance, refurbishment, rent, etc. Village Halls, medium sized monthly meeting groups, Churches, sports groups, Community Centres etc. Not suitable for children.

Expected return: 50% of cash collected. i.e. £600 per annum for monthly £1.00 stake from 100 club members.

What's in it for contributors: 50% of cash collected given in prizes.

Frequency: On-going with monthly prizes.

Special requirements: Permission to run a Social Lottery. Recognised charity – to raise funds for. See back of the book for details on Lotteries.

Variations on a theme: If you confine your 100 Club to members of a club or society e.g. the PTA for a school or members of a Sunday Cycling club you are exempt from registration; you can only advertise within the confines of your clubhouse or building or private premises of the members but there is no limit to the size of the lottery or on the price of each number.

How does the 100 Club work?

One hundred members pay a joining fee of, say, £2 (or less). The joining fee pays for administration and stationery. Each month they pay a regular amount of £1 (the maximum fee that you are allowed to charge under the restrictions of the present regulations) which entitles them to enter the current month's draw. So far so good.

Now comes the clever bit. The prizes are fairly modest for ten months of the year; £20 for the first prize and £10 for the second. But twice a year, perhaps in June and December the club pays out larger prizes; first prize – £100, second prize – £50. This keeps members interested and prepared to stay in the club for a year or more which makes collecting the contributions easier as you can encourage members to pay six months in advance, and saves the work of finding more members to replace those who fall by the wayside.

How do I start the 100 Club?

First you need to obtain permission from the group for whom you wish to fundraise that they are happy for you to be doing this and, assuming they agree, then write a short constitution. This will outline your objectives and the rules. This can be very simple but must include:

1. A statement recognising the need for registration under the Lotteries Act.
2. Details of the rules of the collection should be included – who is eligible, what is the prize money, what is the stake, when will the draws take place etc.
3. An address for the promoter should be incorporated and, whilst perhaps not strictly necessary, details of the charitable objects should be outlined.

Next you must register with the Local Authority to enable you to run a Social or Societies' Lottery (see separate chapter on Tax, Licences, Rules and Regulations). This will cost you £35 for initial registration with a further £17.50 annual renewal fee.

At this stage you should work out a marketing plan to attract your hundred contributors. It needn't be complicated. Set a timescale, work out your target audience and plan your attack!

Lets look at the three elements. Your timescale could be realistically set at two months, but you can adjust this as you go: you only need to collect your first month's contributions and draw your first prizewinners when you have about seventy-five percent of the numbers allocated. (Just leave the spare numbers out of the draw and remember to reduce your prizes accordingly or you will find you are short of funds. You must tell your members that you will be changing the prizes, however).

Your target audience will be people living in the locality; all in one village, one parish, or a specific area of a town or city. They will probably be active members of the community and might well be users (or potential users) of the organisation or premises which your 100 Club represents. Don't waste time and effort on people too far from your area or those whose main activities are out of the locality.

Your main attack should use several weapons. Posters (these can be handmade) in shops, pubs, community centres or village halls, column inches in local newsletters or even the local press, possible door-to-door mail shots in the form of a letter. And last but by no means least, the good, old fashioned grapevine. Word of mouth is one of the strongest local advertising media you have available. Start a rumour and see how quickly it gets repeated back to you!

> **HANDY HINT**
> A contributor could, of course, hold two or more numbers and still be legal. But you might like to put your own rules on this to make the chance of a win more even.

Do I have to be fundraising for charity?

Yes. The terms of the Lotteries and Amusements Act specify that you must be an established group and raising money for charitable purposes and this has not changed within the boundaries of the new National Lottery Act 1993.

Are there any other restrictions in the terms of the Act?

Indeed. The total value of chances sold must not exceed £20,000 for any one lottery. Effectively, although the arrangements are exactly the same for each draw, you will be running a separate lottery each month so (sadly!) you will be well within the limits. You do not have to accumulate your proceeds until, say, the end of the year. You may not allocate numbers to children under the age of 16. Perhaps most restrictive of all is that £1.00 is the maximum price that you can ask for each monthly contribution for each number. Finally you will have to make a return, on a form provided, at the end of each year to the Local Authority.

Is the above information correct under the new regulations of the National Lottery Act 1993?

Not necessarily. Although the Act is law from December 1993 some associated regulations have not been issued. As yet we are all obliged to work under the existing legislation where the new rules have not yet been published.

We know that there will be changes to registration requirements, ticket prices and values, prize amounts and expenses allowed; see back of the book for more details. If you have any worries, speak to the Licensing Department of your local authority.

Is the joining fee an annual fee?

Because there will inevitably be people dropping out for any number of reasons you will probably find that the small but steady flow of joining fees will cover the very minimal costs of membership cards, stationery etc. If you are not covering costs you might have to consider increasing the initial fee or making it an annual one.

What if people are late paying up?

You should make it clear in the rules that accompany each member's card, that numbers will not be included in the draw if funds have not been received PRIOR to that draw taking place.

How is the Club and its promoters kept free from suspicion?

You should have two operators – though this is not required by law; the Promoter and an Hon. Treasurer is the usual set up. You will probably be a branch group from a larger organisation (the one for whom you are raising funds) and will benefit from a committee overseeing your activities.

The draw should take place on a completely separate occasion, perhaps a monthly meeting of another local group, and by people who are not members of the 100 Club.

Your accounts should be brought up to date each month and be available for examination at any time if required.

It helps if winners names are published, perhaps quarterly. The list could be made available to contributors only, but if it can be displayed on a notice board of the local Community Centre it will act as a powerful marketing tool if you need more contributors.

Possible problems?

You may not be able to use this method for raising church funds as many church groups do not like the idea of gambling. The 100 Club is certainly a game of chance and so by definition is a form of gambling. By the same token you may be restricted from advertising the Club in the local Parish newspaper, a useful source of readers; on the church hall notice board; or from having the draw at a Church function.

If you cannot find your full quota of members within a reasonable time and you are forced to start your draws giving reduced prizes, make sure that all the members know in advance that this might happen by including this option in the rules. You don't want to be accused of changing things as you go along.

PLUS & MINUS

- + Continuous source of funding
- + No venue necessary
- + Advertising not usually needed after the initial drive
- + Know your monthly income

- − Relies on continuous help from several people
- − Can't operate if too many people drop out
- − Might not be suitable for certain groups due to gambling associations
- − Need licence
- − Late payments from collector to promoter mean some contributors' numbers will not be in a draw (or the draw delayed if this is allowed in the rules).

EVENT 15

JUMBLE SALES

Second-hand clothes sale

Operating requirements: A co-ordinator and a treasurer. Somebody or some people who are prepared to collect or have jumble delivered to their homes for weeks prior to your date. On the day you will need at least one helper for each table and two others to take money. If you have loads of extra jumble you might need another 'floating' helper to keep adding to the piles from a stock kept elsewhere.

Equipment needs: A hall or room. Trestle tables according to the size of your sale. Wheeled clothes rails, if possible. Somewhere safe to keep the money. Large quantities of carrier bags for Variation 2. Blackboards or sign boards for Variation 3.

Lead time: At least a month, possibly two.

Initial cost: Cost of hire of room and publicity.

Suitable for: Every type of organisation.

Expected return: Probably less than £100.

What's in it for customers and helpers: Customers get a chance to buy, often very good, clothes at silly prices and they don't have to go into town for them. It's a chance for a bit of a chin-wag and gives people an opportunity to get rid of stuff that they feel is a sin to throw out. Jumble Sales appeal to our conscience. Actually I hate Jumble Sales so I have to be severely pressured to help, but there are those who like nothing better than to see a pile of clothes disappear in a mad rush of elbows and handbags. And there are, of course, helpers' perks which mean that they get the pick of the stock before the doors open (for a price, naturally). I did once come by a beautiful woollen winter coat in this way.

Frequency: As long as you weed the real junk from your jumble you can hold a Jumble Sale as and when you have enough for a sale. If you keep turning out the same grotty clothes every time your customers will soon decide that there is better to be had somewhere else.

How does it work?

Old clothes are donated regularly to a known collector. When enough is collected, a sale is held, usually in a public building. Nobody really needs to be told what happens at a Jumble Sale; there can't be anyone in the country who has never been to one. Except, possibly, the Queen. I bet even she would like one visit, if only to see who bought her Hermes head scarves! However, there are three variations on running a Sale. You might find one idea more suited to your needs than the others.

How do I get started?

First check that the group or charity that you are collecting for isn't holding a rival event in the locality. Send the word out that you are collecting jumble; you can decide on a date for the actual sale at this stage or later if you wish.

The easiest method of starting the grapevine working is to pin a notice in a couple of local shops or newsagents. Put a couple of lines into the community newspaper or get the charity or group themselves to pass the word at a meeting or gathering.

Book a date at the hall you plan to use and start to advertise your Sale within about two or three weeks of the date. If you have a mountain of clothes to shift you might consider placing a small classified advertisement in your area's newspaper, otherwise you can rely on local posters in the school, the hall itself or shops. These sort of events do tend to sell themselves, especially once you have established a reputation, but you can't rely on it. Most independent radio stations have a free listing of all local charity events, so make sure you drop them a line giving all the salient facts and not forgetting to include your name and contact number in case they want more details.

As it arrives, sort your jumble into different sections; shoes, hats, outdoor-wear, sports clothes, jumpers and men's and women's clothes. Children's and babies' clothes should be sorted by age or size. You may decide to keep all obviously summery or wintery clothes aside until a more suitable season. Another popular section is a dressing-up box where really dotty items can go, all for 5p each. Make sure the clothes are clean. Some people donate jumble in a truly appalling state. Decide if it is worth washing and if not, chuck it away. It is rarely worth having something dry-cleaned unless you are saving it for a fifty-fifty sale (see Nearly-New Sale section).

What happens on the day?

Make sure that you have lots of helpers available. Start in the morning and lay your room out slowly so that you are not under pressure. Ask, at this stage, for volunteers to return after the sale is over to help pack the remainder away and tidy up. Let them know how long you think it will take. Provide some refreshments for your helpers and lock up securely when you all go to lunch. If you can't secure the hall or room, you will have to leave a couple of people to look after things until you return.

Traditionally Jumble Sales start at 2.00pm, so make sure your table helpers and money takers arrive a quarter of an hour before opening. Run through your plans so that everyone is clear what to do and give them an idea how long they will have to stay at the end.

Sales in my area tend to be short and furious, usually everything is all over in about an hour or an hour and a half at most. I'm sure other parts of the country are the same. Don't drag the thing out unless you have very good items and provide a creche. (You can advertise this as a Nearly New Sale and always publicise added attractions such as a creche or tea.)

Arrange your tables in two lines using two further tables to join the lines at top and bottom to form a long rectangle. Pile your jumble in

PLUS & MINUS

- ⊞ Great way to get rid of old clothes.
- ⊞ All over fairly quickly.
- ⊞ Doesn't need serious marketing or costly publicity.
- ⊞ Nearly New Sales can be successful fundraisers.
- ⊞ Needs no special equipment other than tables and possibly a clothes rail.
- ⊟ You will need to hire a room or public building.
- ⊟ Jumble Sales can attract some intimidating people.
- ⊟ Jumble sales are not very lucrative unless you establish a real reputation for quality.
- ⊟ You will almost certainly lose a certain amount due to theft.
- ⊟ You need space to store jumble and might be left with piles that you have to get rid of.

sections around the table. Place the clothes rails, if you have them (they are sometimes available for a nominal price from department stores), around the end of the room furthest from the door. People tend to browse through these and you don't want to cause a bottle neck near the entrance. Where there is a stage put the hats, shoes and dressing-up box here if you are short of space. In each area ensure that you have at least one helper per table or rail. On the main table, helpers work inside the rectangle; from here they can keep a good eye on what is going on.

You can charge an entrance fee but I feel it is better not to. On the other hand you might have a tradition of charging for entrance in your area, in which case it is probably better not to rock the boat by changing things.

Variation 1: The traditional jumble sale involves bargaining with a helper, agreeing a price and handing over the money. It helps if all the helpers taking money are wearing money aprons. They won't have the time or space to keep searching for change in a communal box and they should keep their eyes on the tables at all times.

Variation 2: I favour this method and it is a real cracker for jumble that has been around a while or is seriously out of fashion. As each customer enters they are given several carrier bags and told that they can fill the bags with anything they like. All carriers are charged £1.00 at the exit.

Variation 3: This method is good for difficult areas (see Problems below). Work out a pricing structure prior to your event i.e. Jumpers and skirts – 50p, trousers – 75p, babies clothes – 25p etc. Display the prices on black boards around the room so that helpers and customers can see them. As customers leave the hall they are fed through a funnel made from two or four tables where the goods are priced and charged. There is no debate and no arguments. You may be left with quite a lot of grot but you can hold a pound-a-bag sale for the last half hour if you feel brave.

If you have heaps of serious rubbish to get rid of, bag it all up yourselves, put a £10 note in one bag and advertise the fact and, as before, sell each bag for £1.00.

NEARLY NEW SALE

A nearly new or 50/50 sale is run largely on Jumble Sale lines so I feel that it doesn't really warrant a whole chapter to itself.

The main difference is that instead of the price for each item being recorded as profit, you are committed to returning a percentage of the sale price to the original owner. In effect you are charging commission to sell something on behalf of someone else. You are likely to receive clothes in much better condition than for jumble sales, but they will be priced correspondingly higher. You can insist that all clothes are freshly laundered or cleaned and intact with buttons and fastenings firmly secured.

Usually the percentage is fifty percent, but it could be anything you choose. In our area we find that we can only get a reasonable quantity of good quality clothes if we offer a sixty/forty split – donors keep the sixty percent. And, of course, it doesn't have to be restricted to clothes. No-longer-needed baby equipment is always popular, it has such a short period of use that unless you go in for vast families it is unlikely to wear out. Gardening tool and equipment nearly-new sales are also popular, especially at fetes. Toys, household goods, curtains and furniture are all worth thinking about.

But how do you know who owned what?

For garden tools which sell reasonably slowly over the counter you can keep a written record and tick things off as you sell them. This is obviously totally impractical when you are selling clothes in a village hall in the scrum as described above.

The simplest method is to get all owners to price up their own goods. The sale price is written on the front of a square of paper and the name is written on the back (it could include a telephone number if owners are not well known to the organisers) and pinned to each item using a safety pin (dressmaker's pins come off and can injure people).

The sale is conducted in exactly the same way as Variation 3 except that each item is priced individually as explained above. When the cashiers take the money they remove the labels and drop them into a tub. When everything is all over, the remaining clothes are sorted into piles according to the owner, the labels from the sold clothes are also sorted into piles. Sixty percent of the accumulative value of those items sold is given to the owner when they come to collect any remaining clothes. In this way you sort out all the finances there and then and are not left with piles of clothes to return.

Possible problems?

Loads of 'em! Jumble Sales attract a unique type of customer. You will find them lined up at every sale at least half an hour before opening time. They tend to be large women dressed in dark Macs, whatever the weather, and carry huge bags. They seem to possess more than their fair share of elbows and move like lightning.

Beware though, although most of your customers will be genuinely looking for bargains, and some may be in dire need of anything that you can offer, there will be others who come to steal. I have been told of people who arrive with bags ready prepared with false bottoms! When challenged they are abusive, obnoxious and deny everything. They will look at you with an eye as unnerving as a goat's and let forth a stream of personal comments that make you want to give them everything you have just so they go away. That is their plan. If your sales habitually attract this 'element' as my Granny would say, you might be better off using Variation 3 or you will begin to lose volunteers and a good proportion of your customers.

HANDY HINT

Go in for a bit of home-made security. I'm not suggesting that you employ Securicor, but a tall man dressed in dark trousers, a blue shirt and sporting some very shiny shoes does wonders for moral!

A further problem is what to do with the piles of real junk that you cannot sell. Oxfam, Age Concern, or Sue Ryder will not be interested in them any more than you are, so don't embarrass charity shops into having to refuse your rubbish. If you have any out-of-style, but good condition, men's suits or outdoor coats that you just can't get shot of, they might be interested.

You can try any recycling companies that you find in your local yellow pages, but you will have to deliver and they will probably only give you about a couple of pounds per hundredweight. You might think it is worth it. Some rag companies take duff jumble but only if you remove all buttons, zips etc. You may be left having to take it to a municipal dump, which seems criminal but maybe the only option.

EVENT 16

KARAOKE NIGHT

Volunteers sing-along to a backing track

Operating requirements: Co-ordinator, treasurer. Compere and road crew who should come with the equipment.

Equipment needs: Screens and sound system, risers or stage area. Video camera and blank tapes.

Lead time: Three months, depending on the availability of the equipment.

Initial cost: Under £50, unless you plan to hire a hall and do your own event from scratch.

Suitable for: Any charity that is youth based or wishes to raise awareness within the under 25s.

Expected return: Karaoke is not a guaranteed fundraiser. If you judge your market carefully and exploit every angle the idea has good potential.

What's in it for contributors: A chance for a really good laugh, companionable entertainment and an opportunity to participate rather than retiring to the usual position of anonymous spectator in the dark. Particularly good in villages where there is little else in the form of live entertainment.

Frequency: The more often the better. Appreciation and confidence grows with experience.

Special requirements: Your venue must be licenced for Public Entertainment. Unless you are aiming at under 16s you will also need a Liquor Licence.

What is Karaoke?

Karaoke came from Japan about ten years ago, where participation entertainment is much more part of the culture. It provides an opportunity for ordinary people, having had no musical background, to get up in front of an audience and sing live whilst being accompanied by pre-recorded music.

Ten years ago a Karaoke evening consisted of a microphone and some instrumental-only records of popular songs, often as part of a disco. It has come a long way since then and you should not consider hiring any Karaoke equipment that does not provide several TV screens, use video discs with sophisticated sound equipment and have enough microphones to cover a group of six or more.

It is unusual to find Karaoke other than in a pub these days, but if you choose to hire a public hall you will be well advised to have a bar as well. We Brits are known for our reserved behaviour and a good slug of alcohol is often needed to lubricate the vocal chords...at least at the beginning of the evening. Although you might find it difficult to draw the evening to a close once your participants have shaken off the manacles of shyness...

How can I use Karaoke to fundraise?

Karaoke is not cabaret, although it can be used to complement a cabaret evening, but unless you are brave enough to organise a whole cabaret show you probably should not consider hiring a hall and selling tickets. After all, why should people pay to take part when they can have regular Karaoke entertainment in their local for free?

No, the way to maximise your proceeds from Karaoke is to go to the places where it is already taking place on a regular basis. Fundraising is achieved by exploiting the evening without spoiling the informal atmosphere and there are several methods that you can use, but for all ideas you should aim for the following elements.

You need an audience that you can rely on and one that has already conquered inherent inhibitions. You need a venue that is used to hosting the evening and already holds the various licences that you are required to have by law. And you need a popular Karaoke compere who uses modern equipment. Spend a few weekends travelling around experiencing different Karaoke pubs until you find one that you like. Then start cultivating the landlord!

Raise money by adding to the entertainment rather than detracting from it or changing the original idea. Try selling videos of the singers. Buy or cadge video tapes (they need only be about 15 minutes in length) find a camcorder hot-shot to record each singer and sell the tapes for £5.00 at the end. Make sure that you put every 'turn' from each singer onto the same tape.

Hold a raffle, for donated prizes. A collection taken two or three times during the evening can be successful as can a permanent box left on the bar. You could also try negotiating a percentage of the bar take over and above the average return. Your extra publicity should help to swell usual numbers.

If you find someone very talented that the audience really likes listening to, you could run a Dutch Auction (see relevant chapter) to 'buy' a selection of songs.

Ask to speak to the regular compere at your chosen venue. Pick his brains for ideas and get him on your side. He (or she) will know his audience best of all and might well be very enthusiastic if he is involved at the planning stage. He might even be prepared to run a competition (paid entries, of course) for the best compere if he doesn't feel too threatened. The winner gets to compere the next half-hour or whatever.

Some organisations have tried to fundraise by running Karaoke competitions. 'It don't work', as I was informed succinctly by one Karaoke compere. It fundamentally changes the atmosphere from one where a singer can make a fool of himself and the audience are good natured enough to take it all in good part until the next turn, to a feeling of serious competition, often from outsiders, all aiming to win cash or a holiday. People complain of unfairness, claim that they need another go or just won't even bother coming if they feel they are not much good.

HANDY HINT

Look in the What's On column of your local newspaper to discover which pubs feature Karaoke.

Will I need to advertise?

Although the pub will undoubtedly have its own marketing policy, you should offer to undertake some additional publicity.

Find out where they already advertise; you don't want to duplicate efforts, and major on the fact that you will be offering something special such as the videos, for instance. Sell the event to the press by using the charity angle. If you know someone in the business, consider persuading a well known singer to open the evening or to sing along with people. You will sell many more videos this way. Even a popular footballer or other young sports person might be willing to help.

So, yes, you need to publicise. Though maybe you need to look more at PR rather than straight advertisements.

Is it all songs from the charts?

There is a good selection of golden oldies, such as Frank Sinatra and the Beatles which many older people enjoy singing to. There are also some traditional folk songs and a good choice of country and blue grass music that can all be used to theme an evening, although it has to be said that the main selection is from the '90s.

However, tucked away in some videodisc catalogues you can find 'Roll out the Barrel' and other war time classics. You could try putting together an over 60s Karaoke night using all the old songs. If you are old enough to remember singing round the pub piano or have seen smoky pub sing-songs in all those old Elstree studio movies you'll know that there is a great untapped talent out there who are used to community singing and might be longing to have a go.

Possible problems?

The beauty of using a Karaoke pub is that any problems that there might be are not yours. The landlord should sort out any rowdiness and the compere is there to direct the singers. All you have to do is exploit the situation. In the best possible taste, of course!

On the other hand, if you get a pub full of people like me, you'll never persuade any of them to get up and sing. And you wouldn't want to anyway!

PLUS & MINUS

- + If you use a pub you will need very little outlay or help.
- + It is one of the few fundraising ideas that really appeals to the 18 – 25 year age group.
- + Could be good at changing the image of a largely middle age, middle class charity to give it a broader appeal.
- + It can be held on a regular basis.
- + You take advantage of a ready made audience.
- − Bit hit and miss when it comes to raising money.
- − Not suitable for children.
- − No good if you are looking for an event without alcohol.

EVENT 17

PROMISE AUCTION

A sale of promises of duties

Operating requirements: Co-ordinator/Auctioneer, Treasurer, steward/clerk, cashier/s.

Equipment needs: This activity is most successful when held on the back of another event (see Dutch Auction) so equipment and furniture may already be available. Chairs for the audience and a podium/soap box or stage. A means of making a record of the bids and collecting cheques or cash. About fifty 'promises', this will take just over an hour to get through. You could hold the event in its own right and sell catalogues (see Dutch Auction), sell refreshments or have a bar.

Lead time: A month or six weeks for a small auction, up to twelve weeks if you anticipate a grander show.

Initial cost: Very little outlay. A contribution, perhaps to the publicity of the main event.

Suitable for: Very local events for local causes. Ideal or raising money for schools, churches, local groups or issues.

Expected return: Over £100 – £500, depending on the quality of your promises and the generosity of your audience.

What's in it for contributors: Opportunity to buy a service that might otherwise be unavailable or prohibitively expensive. Adds to the enjoyment of another event. Donors have an opportunity to support a special cause in a way other than financial.

Frequency: Annual. Choose a time when people feel flush or in need of some help. Christmas time or the start of the Summer holidays, perhaps.

Special requirements: An experienced and lively auctioneer. If you have a bar you will need to be licenced.

Variations on a theme: Slave auction, Surprise auction, Silent auction, Sealed-Bid auction. Details at the end of the chapter.

How does it work?

The auction is run on identical lines to a conventional auction. It is the lots that are different. Each lot is a 'Promise', usually typed on individual sheets of paper, signed by the person making the promise and sealed in an envelope.

Just use your imagination, ask around, collect donations from commercial companies, leisure centres, farmers, your local MP. The list is endless. Make sure you have a good choice from handmade goods, special opportunities, offers of help and donated items.

How do I get started?

Gather a small group of helpers or form a committee. Decide on a date and a venue and apply for an occasional liquor licence if you are to have a bar.

Your next priority is finding an auctioneer. Because this event is run on traditional lines a professional auctioneer will bring a touch of reality as well moving the bidding along fast and keeping the patter going. If someone local wants to have a go they need to have a 'presence', keep calm and have a few trial runs before the day. I really do recommend the professional as it is stressful work keeping up the pace for the whole show.

At this stage you need to go looking for your donations and promises. Try to get specific commitments from people. It is not enough to get a vague 'Oh, all right then'. Type up the promises and get them signed before the donor can back out. Make it clear that each offer of help is kept open for a year only.

What do we do on the day?

Prepare your room as in the Dutch Auction. Place the cashiers desk at the back and arrange to have it staffed all the time, not just at the end, to avoid queues. Hand out or sell a catalogue or list of all the lots so that people can study them before the bidding begins. (If you are running the event in it's own right, you can sell refreshments for half-an-hour or so before the start to enable people to buy and study their catalogues). Set a target at the beginning of the auction and announce that you hope to collect this by the end of the evening. Every now and then you can interject with the running total to keep the incentive going.

As each lot is sold the clerk should make a note of the name of the winning bidder and a steward should pass them a slip to be exchanged at the cashier's desk.

During the auction you can sell drinks and snacks from a waiter/ waitress service. This prevents the disruption of a constant stream of people getting up to visit the bar.

Variations

Surprise auction. To add a bit of spice, keep three popular lots in unmarked envelopes, let it be known that the next lot is one of the three things, but you don't know which! People make blind bids and get a surprise at the end. Don't announce what each lot is until all have been bought.

Silent auction: If there are too many lots to get through you can hold a Silent Auction alongside the Promise Auction or Dutch Auction. Display details of each lot and the reserve on blackboards or on large sheets of card on the tables. Bids are written alongside together with the name and address of each bidder. Leave plenty of space to allow bids

PROMISES MIGHT INCLUDE:

- 2 x hours gardening
- 1 x morning child minding
- 1 x home-made cake
- Handyman for a day
- Trip in a boat
- Free meal at a pub
- 4 x pantomime tickets
- 2 x sessions baby-sitting
- Meal cooked in your house
- Football coaching
- Housework
- Cleaning cars
- Decorate a room
- A day's fishing
- A round of golf with a professional
- A week's holiday in a country cottage
- A free make-over at the local beautician
- Tour of the local fire station
- One day's produce from allotment

HANDY HINT

It helps if you publish a reserve price to give people an idea of where to start the bidding.

PLUS & MINUS

- ⊞ Popular and unusual idea.
- ⊞ People like to donate services.
- ⊞ Good PR. The memory of the auction and the cause is kept alive as people redeem their promises throughout the year.
- ⊞ Needs no special equipment.
- ⊞ Can piggyback on another event.

- ⊟ Does rely on the quality of your auctioneer.
- ⊟ Can be hard work and time-consuming collecting promises.
- ⊟ Not suitable for children.

to be crossed out and replaced several times. See that new bids are higher than the ones they replace!

Sealed-Bid auction: Display the lots as above and make pens, paper and envelopes available. Bidders place bids in sealed envelopes and place them in a box. The winners are announced at the end. Proceeds are usually lower for this method.

Slave auction: All the lots are promises of services. So your 'slave' might offer to cut your lawn every week for a month, or cook a meal every weekend in August or chauffeur you about for a morning.

What happens at the end?

Try to persuade all bidders to pay for and collect their lots, where appropriate, on the spot.

Make sure that you thank your auctioneer; present him or her with a bunch of flowers or a bottle of something.

Ensure that you have arranged for some volunteers to help you clear up.

Afterwards, write thank you letters to commercial donors, your auctioneer and all who acted as stewards or clerks and cashiers on the night. Make sure that you publish how much you raised in the local newspaper or on a local notice board. People like to know that an event they supported was a success and those that couldn't make it might be prepared to come next time.

Possible problems?

Occasionally you might have a dispute between bidders; make it clear that the auctioneer has the final discretion.

You may feel it necessary to announce that your group accepts all donations in good faith and does not accept liability for bad workmanship or faulty goods. There is no exchange or refund.

EVENT 18

RAFFLES, TOMBOLAS AND SWEEPSTAKES

All you never knew you needed to know!

I have arranged this chapter a little differently to most of the other fundraising ideas collected in this book. Games of chance are governed strictly by law and I feel some general explanation is warranted before the 'recipe' is given.

There cannot be anyone reading this book who has not at some time been a participant in a raffle or tombola, unless they are a member of a particular religious or ethical group that does not agree with the element of gambling involved. Virtually every event uses one of the two to swell funds and encourage the public to stay a little longer and spend a little more money. Many people will be so familiar with the workings of both as to skip this chapter altogether. If you are not inclined to read further, may I please suggest that you at least turn to the chapter on Tax, Licences, Rules and Regulations to satisfy yourself that what you plan is legal.

Good fun and lucrative as they are, raffles, tombolas and sweepstakes are all a form of gambling, they are all games of chance and as such come under the Lotteries and Amusements Act 1976 and the new National Lottery Act 1993 which came into force at the end of 1993.

There are, broadly speaking, three types of lotteries, being those which are private, small or social. Each has different levels of regulation. For our purposes, i.e. charitable and fundraising organisations, almost all raffles and tombolas will be either private or small if they are to be part of another fundraising event. (See chapter on Tax, Licences, Rules and Regulations for full definitions.)

So what's the difference between a raffle and a tombola?

I believe the border line to have become a little fuzzy over the years. But as I see it, a raffle is the opportunity to buy tickets, or chances, to win one of a small selection of prizes. The draw for these prizes is usually held at the end of a specified period of time. A tombola, on the other hand, works by selling tickets as before, but the draw is made from a revolving drum (tombolare – to somersault, for those who are interested) by the player at the time of purchase. The prizes tend to be more numerous and of a more modest nature.

Both tombolas and raffles have their places. Tombolas are useful at fetes and fairs or other events where the public are passing through. Names and telephone numbers need not be taken and the business is wound up then and there. Raffles are particularly suited to dinner dances or other events where you hang on to your audience for a length of time, at the work place or within a club where the same people meet over a period of days or weeks. Over a longer period of time and for large prizes where you are opening your raffle to the general public you will need a lottery licence. But that is a very different kettle of fish and you can read about Social Lotteries in the specialist chapter as mentioned above.

What about a sweepstake?

Sweepstakes are rather different and consist of a private gamble on the outcome of a public event. In other words a group of people, quite independent from commercial betting shops, decide to bet amongst themselves on the forecast of an event totally out of their control such as the Grand National or the General Election, for instance.

In the main, I feel that sweepstakes are not very useful fundraising tools. They are confined to work within the remit of a private lottery which means that you can only use them within your club or work place, because you are playing for cash. Furthermore, a sweepstake is only a true 'sweep' when all the stakes go to make up the prizes, which doesn't really help your fundraising operation. You could, collectively, make a decision to play for fifty percent of the stakes but you might as well just make a donation for the few pounds that it will bring in.

RAFFLES

Operating requirements: 2 or 3 (or more) people selling tickets.

Equipment needs: Book of numbered tickets with stubs. For a raffle that runs for longer than one event and takes place within a club i.e. a private lottery, your tickets need to bear the price of each ticket and the name and address of the promoter. Small lotteries can use cloakroom tickets.

Lead time: A week or two to collect the prizes.

Initial cost: A couple of pounds for cloakroom tickets. £30-£40 for specially printed tickets.

Suitable for: All charities but check that they are not averse to gambling.

Expected return: If your prizes are donated, all proceeds bar cost of the tickets and perhaps a site fee is yours.

What's in it for contributors: People love a chance to win something for very little. The gambling instinct, if you like.

Special requirements: Study the specialist chapter to ensure that you know your legal position.

Variations on a theme: Numbered programmes – programmes display a 'lucky number' on the front and the draw is made at the end of the event. Programmes can double as entry tickets or be sold separately. Don't forget to sell advertising space to boost funds. 'Guess the birthday of a soft toy.' The toy is the prize. People write a date on a ticket which is then put into a draw. The date and the name of the player is recorded in a diary (thus ensuring that two people cannot choose the same date).

What is the best way to sell tickets?

Make a good display of all your prizes near the entrance so that people can gain enthusiasm, and place one ticket seller beside the display to keep an eye on it. Disperse your other sellers into the crowd to keep walking and asking. The secret of selling raffle tickets is to approach people while they have their purses out. Remember to make a note of people's names, and a contact number if you don't know everyone, on the stub unless you are sure that everyone will be present at the draw. Some raffles operate on a 'strictly present' basis, i.e. if nobody comes forward to claim the ticket another number is drawn.

As soon as one book is empty return it to the co-ordinator (at the stand) to fold up the stubs and start getting the draw ready. For a big raffle you could be tearing and folding for ages unless you do this as you go.

Announce the draw 15 minutes before it is made to enable last minute sales; use a VIP or a neutral person to draw the first ticket. The winner then draws the next ticket and so on. Prizes can be allocated on a first, second, and third basis or winners can be free to choose whatever they like from the selection.

TOMBOLAS

Operating requirements: 2 people selling tickets.

Equipment needs: Book of numbered tickets with stubs. Cloakroom tickets are fine. Spinning drum which you can make or hire from specialist companies (addresses at the back of the book). You can, of course, use any container that you can seal and give a good shake.

Lead time: A week or two to collect the prizes.

Initial cost: A couple of pounds for cloakroom tickets. Suitable for: all charities and most events, but check again that the organisation is not averse to gambling.

Expected return: If your prizes are donated, all proceeds bar cost of the tickets and perhaps a site fee is yours.

What's in it for contributors: Again, people love a chance to win something for very little and in this case they can see immediately if they are a winner.

Special requirements: None as long as you stick to running tombolas at other one-off events and the value of all your prizes at the event is under £250.

Variations on a theme: Alcoholic bottle stall. Non-alcoholic bottle stall. Groceries stall. Fruit stall.

How does it work?

Each prize has a number taped to it in an obvious place. Usually the numbers used are those that end in a zero or a five to make for easy detection. The companion ticket is folded small, so the number is not visible, and put into a container or drum. Biscuit tins are an ideal alternative as you can put a lid on if the wind threatens to blow a cloud of confetti into the air. Now throw away all the other five or zero numbers to avoid confusion. Fold up the rest of the tickets and place them with the others into the drum. Mix them well.

The player pays a set price for five tickets or gets eleven tickets for the price of ten. If a ticket ending in a five or zero is drawn you know they have won a prize.

If you are including alcohol, children under 16 should not be allowed to buy or sell tickets. You might be able to buy bottles from an off-licence on sale or return which can help your overheads.

Is there anything special about a fruit stall?

Several attractively prepared boxes of fruit, ranging in size from, say, a few apples and pears or a large bunch of grapes, a couple of kiwi fruit and a hand of bananas right up to a large presentation pack including melons, a pineapple and a pile of other fruit all make good prizes. Prepare the tickets in just the same way as above.

Ideally the fruit should be covered in some way. If you use clingfilm it can sweat in hot weather unless you punch a few holes in it but in any case you should find a shady spot for your stall.

A fruit stall is often very popular and there are obviously no restrictions on who can buy tickets. You might be able to find a friendly greengrocer to donate the fruit or sell it to you at a discount.

Possible problems?

Bottle Stalls and Fruit Stalls are classified as 'small lotteries' and do not need registration. However accumulative prizes, from all the stalls at the event – not just one type of stall – should not exceed £250. Although this has been increased from £50 to £250 under the new regulations it is still pretty restrictive. Personally I don't think that I have visited any event of a reasonable size that does not flout this regulation. I have never heard of organisers of any fete being prosecuted under the Act, but you should be aware that you might well be breaking the law.

If you are offering food or drink on a Tombola stall check the 'use by' dates carefully and don't offer anything that isn't tinned, boxed, bottled or dry goods in a packet. You are liable under the Food Safety Regulations even though you are not offering goods for sale as such.

PLUS & MINUS

- ⊞ Very little outlay, organisation or staff.
- ⊞ Suits every pocket.
- ⊞ Very good to boost funds at other events.
- ⊞ Good variations to suit a variety of ages and events.
- ⊟ Restrictive where the cumulative value of prizes is concerned.
- ⊟ Be careful that you operate the right kind of 'lottery' at the right event.

EVENT 19

SAFARI DINNER

A meal with courses taken in different venues

Operating requirements: Co-ordinator, Treasurer and 3 hosts.

Equipment needs: Enough chairs, tables, crockery and cutlery. Mode of transport if too far to walk. Suitable means of keeping food hot if necessary.

Lead time: 8 weeks minimum

Initial cost: Cost of ingredients and invitations only.

Suitable for: Small but continuous fundraising. Good in rural areas where there is not much ready entertainment.

Expected return: Work on a 200% mark up on the cost of ingredients, the same as restaurants. Then subtract the minor costs of invitation cards and postage.

What's in it for guests: An enjoyable evening out, a chance to meet some new friends, and the opportunity for someone who enjoys cooking to take part but without the worry of producing a whole meal.

Frequency: This idea is equally suited to the 'one-off' or as a regular date for the same bunch of friends.

Variations on a theme: Cycle Safari – for the environmentally conscious where all the guests have to travel via bicycle. (Safety note – make sure all guests wear safety helmets and reflective bands especially at night.) Picnic Safari – you don't have to travel from spot to spot, but everyone brings part of the picnic. Safari Luncheon. Safari Children's Tea-Party – choose a park or a field and let the children go to a special tree for the sandwiches, another area for jelly and yet another for cake. This is a good way to raise money for a Mums and Toddlers Group.

How does it work?

Guests arrive at separate houses for different courses of a dinner party. Tickets are sold in advance via invitation only.

How do we get started?

Find two or three people who are happy to host part of your event in their house and discuss timings, menus and a budget.

You are now ready to prepare a guest list. Divide the list between the hosts to make a good mix. Keep places to a maximum of 20 and a minimum of 8. You will probably need to send out at least a third more invitations than you think you will need. Remember to include the date and time of the first course, the names of the hosts and the addresses for all parts of the dinner, an address or telephone number for the RSVP, the price of the tickets and the name of the charity or group for whom you are fundraising. After a couple of weeks, if you have not heard from people, make a follow up telephone call. It can help if everyone agrees on certain tasks and the main co-ordinator prepares a note to confirm who is doing what. This saves arguments and acts as an 'aide memoire' for others who will all be leading busy lives, and makes sure nothing is forgotten.

How much time can we allow between courses?

Assuming you are holding a three course meal, a good basis to work on is an hour in each place and 15 minutes change over. So, if the first house opens its doors at 7.30pm for drinks and chat, the guests sit down for their starter at 8.00pm and they can move on at 8.30pm. The next host expects his or her guests at 8.45pm, they start their main course straight away and they will probably be ready to push off at 9.45pm. The last host serves the pud at 10.00pm and everyone stays for coffee for as long as they wish. If you decide on just two or four or even five (some meal!) venues you can adjust your times accordingly.

> **HANDY HINT**
>
> Warn your guests when there is 15 minutes before you are due to leave for the next venue. This allows people to finish conversations, dash to the toilet and find coats without feeling too pressurised. If you are getting very behind, telephone the next host to say that you will be late.

What shall we serve?

Well that is really up to you and perhaps the season in which you hold your party. Remember that your guests will sometimes get behind schedule so forget soufflés or other delicately timed creations or food that looks very tired if it is kept warm for any length of time. You want to make some money out of this bit of fun so don't price yourselves out of the market by choosing smoked salmon, quails' eggs and strawberries at Christmas. On the other hand people might feel a bit peeved if they were given a fry-up and chips. (Although certain members of my family would be delighted!)

If guests are all arriving on foot you can serve as much alcohol as you like (work your budget out at two glasses a head or they could 'bring a bottle' to keep costs down) but it is always sensible to remember to have plenty of juice or squash for drivers or for people who just don't like quantities of wine: it is hard to keep tabs on how much you have had to drink when you go from house to house with a fresh glassful each time.

What if I have more than 20 positive replies?

You could suggest to the latecomers that your party is full up now but you will be happy to put their names down for another party in the future; you can even ask them if they would be happy to be a host at a later date. Don't be tempted to have more than 20 guests unless your hosts own baronial halls deep in the countryside with unlimited parking or, if you are certain of fine weather, everyone can be outside and have a barbecue.

Can I use the party to raise more funds?

Sure. Try a raffle. Or if one or more guests play a musical instrument finish the evening with a concert of paid-for requests. Don't forget to ask people to host another party before they go. Get a signature so they can't back out!

PLUS & MINUS

- ⊞ Provides a really good social event with total control over who attends
- ⊞ Can cater for special needs
- ⊞ Very flexible
- ⊞ Popular
- ⊞ Can include the whole family

- ⊟ Not a real money-spinner, but it helps if people bring a bottle or even contribute some food
- ⊟ Restricted numbers except in special circumstances
- ⊟ Can become a little chaotic unless tightly organised

Possible problems?

If you do not restrict ticket sales to private invitation only you will have to apply for a liquor licence.

Make sure that each venue has adequate parking and that all the guests know how to get there.

If someone has drunk too much to drive home safely make sure that a lift is available.

EVENT 20

SNOWBALL PARTY

A party where the guests hold more parties

Operating requirements: Initial host/hostess, treasurer.

Equipment needs: Nothing other than a persuasive letter writing technique.

Lead time: 2 weeks to prepare the first party. 5 weeks to run the appeal.

Initial cost: Just a few pounds for stationery, postage and refreshments.

Suitable for: Human interest causes.

Expected return: Potentially hundreds of pounds.

What's in it for contributors: Feel-good factor plus an informal get-together with friends. Very good for parents with young children, or retired people.

Frequency: You should only have to use this idea once. If your area has already had a Snowball party going around then leave it for at least a year.

Variations on a theme: Pyramid party. Same idea, just works from back to front. i.e. First host holds a huge party of 50 or more guests. Guests invite half the original amount until it gets down to lots of parties of just two. Some organisations prefer this method as it peters out naturally without having to put a time limit.

How does it work?

The principle is thc same as for a chain letter. OK, suppress your prejudices and I will explain!

You hold a tea party or a coffee morning for five friends. They each pay a minimum of £2.00 and agree to hold a party each for at least two friends, who pay £2.00 to come and throw a party each for two of their friends and so on...

The parties can go on ad nauseum but in general it is best to publish a date, on the accompanying literature, by which all the fees should be in and you call a halt. There does come a point when everyone has been to at least three parties and there is no one left in the area to ask!

How do I get started?

This idea works best where a few heart strings are being tugged. The most successful Snowball Party I have experienced was launched by a desperate couple who had to raise enough money to send their little boy to America and pay for a life-saving operation within the next six months.

Your initial invitation and accompanying explanatory literature has to be absolutely right. It might even be worth paying for a professional

PLUS & MINUS

- + Very good idea for people with little time to spare.
- + Good return for initial effort.
- + Needs very little outlay.
- + Gives retired people or Mums with toddlers an excuse to socialise and get involved where other projects might be impossible. Good also for the elderly or out of work as there is little outlay needed all round.

- − Quickly goes out of your control.
- − Finite amount of parties that can happen in one area. By week 6 you will expect 80 people to hold a party, which is ridiculous.

PR person or copywriter to prepare it for you. If there are nationally produced pamphlets available to explain a particular condition or situation, so much the better.

At the first party you will be in a very positive position. Your friends will all know you well and be on your side from the start. You will be there to answer questions and be persuasive. The next and subsequent parties will not be so easy.

You could host two or three 'first' parties with people from different areas. In this way you can run consecutive Snowball Parties without the danger that you will run out of guests and you will make double or three times the proceeds.

So how do I ensure that subsequent parties are a success?

Firstly you must make it easy for people to contribute. It is the responsibility of the hostess to collect the fees and send them on to you. She will hand out literature about the cause and invitations to be used for the next parties. Guests can either write to you for more copies of invitations and leaflets or they can opt to photocopy more for themselves. The latter is really the easier.

Make sure you include:- the invitation, with the minimum donation made very clear; a piece about this particular appeal to include the tearjerker, your target figure, how it works, where to send contributions and when it is to stop; a general pamphlet and a thank you note which includes a further invitation to send a larger donation and/or a name and address so that they can be informed of the outcome.

How much could I make from this?

Lets do a few sums based on the premise that the appeal is to run for 5 weeks. Assume that the parties are held weekly and the minimum fee is £2.

Of course, not every guest will hold a party but there will be others that invite more than two and some may donate more than £2, so what you lose on the swings you gain on the roundabouts.

The first party has five guests (= £10). Week 2 and 5 people invite 2 each (=£20). Week 3 and 10 people invite 2 each (=£40). Week 4 and 20 people invite 2 each (=£80). Week 5 and 40 people invite 2 each (=£160). Now add it all up and you have £310. If you have three Snowballs growing at once you can make £930. Good money for letting something largely take care of itself!

EVENT 21 SPONSORED ACTIVITIES

Individuals pledge to collect money for activities achieved

The London Marathon is probably the most well known sponsored event in the UK. It has acquired the kind of reputation and kudos that other race organisers can only dream of. Where else can you expect national television crews to turn out in full for hours on end so that continuous progress can be broadcast and the results reported in all the headline news?

But sponsored events need not be on the grand scale of the London Marathon to achieve a good result. In this section I will go through three ideas in detail, but don't stop there. Use the basic outline to work out your own ideas – you are only restricted by the limits of your own imagination. As well as the more usual sponsored swims, walks and runs, I have heard of sponsored beard shaves, bungee jumping, chess marathons, and group silences. The Norfolk Churches hold a very successful sponsored cycle ride around 60+ churches every summer. Children attempt hopscotch marathons or carol singing. Knitting clubs organise sponsored patches; as well as sponsoring each knitter 2p a square you get the most wonderful patchwork blanket to donate or raffle for further funds. Sponsored orienteers collect money on the amount of seconds they knock off a specific time or the number of posts they manage to record. I have even heard of a sponsored vasectomy! And I know of one brave leukaemia patient who had a sponsored head shave in public just before he went into hospital to undergo a gruelling period of chemotherapy when he was told to expect considerable hair loss anyway. You have to admire someone in such circumstances being able to look on the positive side of something so uncomfortable.

Whilst you should treat each event and activity separately there are, however, some general rules of thumb and tips that can be universally applied.

Collections

Collections taking place in a public place are governed by law and a collection does not have to be money. This means that children, or adults, going from door to door or standing outside a local shop asking people to sign their sponsorship forms is illegal without permission. (See chapter on Street Collections for definitions of public places and how to apply for a permit.) Of course, what you do within a school, office or your own home is your business but make yourselves and your teams aware what is, and what is not, permissible.

Swelling funds

If you number all your sponsorship forms you will be in a position to offer a lucky draw (check the Raffles chapter for Lotteries registration if necessary) for all participants or helpers who return them with more

On the whole you can divide sponsored events into three groups although some can be a mixture of the first and last

- Major events where individuals take part but acquire sponsorship for their own causes. (Such as the London Marathon.)
- Those where individuals or teams who attempt a death defying or extraordinary feat on a unique basis. (A parachute jump or bed push, for instance.)
- A collective event that encourages many people to enter and all raise money for the umbrella cause. (A fun-run is a good example.)

than, say, £5. If your event is in the form of a race you will also be able to log each entrant through the finish and tie up the number that they wear on their vests with the number on the form (see below). Ask a local business to donate a prize for the draw and a prize for the person who raises, and collects, the most sponsorship. These tips help to raise extra funds and give that all important encouragement to people to collect all their pledges.

Suggest that each competing individual gathers a fundraising team of three or four people. S/he can concentrate on the activity, especially if it is something like a marathon which needs training, whilst others concentrate on raising and collecting money.

National or local personalities are very valuable both to start the race or to compete. Let it be known right from the start that your VIP will be racing too and you will gain all sorts of extra entries just so that people can catch a glimpse or the possibility of a chat with the 'star'.

Particularly appropriate entrants often make very successful fundraisers. Think of Keith Castle who ran for charity after his heart transplant. Somebody in their sixties joining a Roller Marathon in aid of Age Concern would gain a lot of support and possible media coverage for your cause, but do be sensitive when asking people to help. The last thing you what is to be seen as blatantly using people for your own ends, however laudable these might be.

Collecting pledges

The onus is on the competitors to collect their own contributions. When you sign the forms to say that they have completed the race or clocked up so many miles, make a note of the total amount promised. I have heard complaints that people can lose interest in collecting their sponsorship after the event and a significant percentage of promised money is never forthcoming. There are ways to overcome this.

1. Make it clear that the total recorded after the race is expected to be paid by the competitor even if s/he does not collect all that is owed. If there is a possibility that money might come out of their own pockets there is a powerful incentive to collect thoroughly.

2. Whilst it is unreasonable to expect a cheque on the day of the actual event, do publish a realistic date for all sponsorship monies to be paid in full. Two to three weeks is reasonable. After this date you can send a reminder letter and possibly make a follow up visit although in the majority of cases this will not be necessary.

3. For a small event give three or four alternative contacts to pass funds and sponsorship forms to. For a large event it is worth while opening a special account at a bank or building society so that competitors can pay money in at their local branch. The cashier stamps the form and the competitor then sends the stamped form to the organiser to prove that payment has been made.

Sponsorship forms

Every form should include the name of the benefiting charity, the name and nature of the event, where and when it is to be held, who is organising the event, a contact address and telephone number, space for the name of the competitor and a statement that indicates that the competitor is responsible for paying the amount totalled (this should be signed by the competitor: failure to sign the form means that it will not be stamped at the end of the event to prove that the activity was completed). Then you need five columns headed, Name of Sponsor, Address, Amount per..., Total, Signature, and at least fifteen blank rows down. At the bottom of the form you need a space to enter the accumulative total, instructions for paying in the money, and the date for the final payment to be made. There should be a space for the official stamp and the final number of laps, or whatever, achieved or completed. If the event has attracted company or Sports Council sponsorship the appropriate declarations and logos should also be included.

PR opportunities

Consider a sponsored race for part of the launch for a new cause. Even if you don't raise thousands of pounds for the appeal it is a very good way of spreading the word and increasing public awareness. You will get ten or a dozen sponsors for each competitor all learning about your cause and passing the word on, aside from the crowds who you hope will attend the actual event.

Armed with some examples of three such ideas you should be able to adjust and temper the advice given above and below to run almost any sponsored event you might care to think of... so on with the details.

BED PUSH MARATHON

Operating requirements: Committee consisting of a co-ordinator, treasurer, secretary, and several other members to assist on the day according to the size of your event. Stewards for the route. First-aider.

Equipment needs: A wheeled bed for each team or insist they supply their own. Collection tins. Fancy dress. Sponsorship forms. Starting tape. Refreshments. First aid kit.

Lead time: 3 to 6 months.

Initial cost: Cost of publicity and printing sponsorship forms. Prizes and medals should be sponsored. For a large event you should be able to attract company sponsorship to pay your administration and publicity costs.

Suitable for: Hospitals, GP's surgeries, Playgroups, Schools, Children's or Illness related charities.

Expected return: This really does depend on how diligent your pushers are at obtaining sponsorship and how much you manage to collect 'en route'.

What's in it for contributors: A thoroughly enjoyable, and competitive, event that is as equally fun to watch as to take part. Sponsors are only relieved that they don't have to join in!

Frequency: Annually in the same area, but you could run more if you change the route, although your sponsors might get a little tired.

Special requirements: A street collection licence from the Local Authority. Police support.

Variations on a theme: Circular Bed Push – takes place over a circular route, perhaps around a park or a pedestrianised city centre, for a specified number of circuits or time.

How does it work?

A team, or teams, of people, often in fancy-dress, push an occupied bed along a prearranged route. Money is collected through sponsorship and by collection alongside the bed or in pubs, or similar, afterwards.

In detail, the 'patient' is pushed for 24 hours or as long as the teams can keep going. You need several teams of at least six people (one in the bed, one on each corner and a collector), who each push and collect for an hour at a time. Sometimes you have competing teams, more often than not it is just the one bed with several teams all working together and taking their turns. The more people you have involved, the more money you will raise. The 'patient' might volunteer to be pushed for the whole 24 hours and attract special sponsorship and media coverage.

Usually a marathon will take place over a circular or roughly a figure of eight course along public roads although you can organise the event like an old- fashioned steeplechase and progress continually along one route. The police may not be too happy about you covering the same route several times, however a Sunday marathon might enable you to use a small city centre route or you could consider a public park as you would a pram race, although this might become rather tedious. The plus point of keeping the whole event fairly compact is that you can make a permanent site for your 'pit stops'.

How do we get started?

Form a committee and contact the police to help work out your route and a date. It may be that they will want to arrange to cone off an area to stop cars parking on the roadside or they might insist that they provide a motorcycle outrider to warn other road users that you are coming. They might say that you can only do it on a Sunday when traffic is at its lightest. Ideally, you will want to use a city-centre for at least part of the route on a Saturday afternoon. Some police forces are very anti-bed pushes due to badly organised events in the past, not only because of congestion but also the risk of accidents on major, but narrow, roads.

You will need to work out your stages very carefully and to supply a support crew. The teams may need a couple of mini vans to transport them when they are resting or having refreshments. You will also need an experienced first aid officer, plenty of food and drink and some planned loo stops.

Make sure that you will be granted a Street Collection Permit for that day. Most local authorities will not allow more than one group collecting in the same area on the same day. (See chapter on Tax, Licences, Rules and Regulations for details.)

At least four weeks – possibly more for a large event – before the event send out an advice sheet and the sponsorship forms.

How do we 'sell' the idea?

Having arranged your route and the date, you are now in a position to start your publicity. You will need to advertise for teams. This might be an in-house 'press gang' operation for a hospital or school or you could advertise through the Chamber of Commerce, pubs or in the newspaper if you are opening the event to the general public. Advertise your prizes to inject some healthy competition between rival teams.

You should also start planning your publicity to ensure that people come out to see the push, to donate money and to raise the level of awareness for your cause.

Whilst you aim for a minimum of six in each team, ideally there should be as many volunteers, who may not be affiliated to a team, as you or they can muster to carry collecting tins or buckets and run alongside. So make sure the call goes out to collectors in your publicity from the beginning.

HANDY HINT

One member of the team can follow behind pushing a wheelbarrow. Buckets get heavy and periodically collectors can empty them into the barrow. Spectators can also throw coins straight into the barrow. This also makes a good 'photo-opportunity' for the press.

PLUS & MINUS

- + Can be a very exciting and profitable event.
- + The event is suitable for families to watch.
- + The marathon is unusual enough to attract media coverage.
- − Probably better not to enter under 12s for the teams.
- − Need support of police.
- − Need Street Collection Licence.

What happens on the day?

Make sure your teams are absolutely sure of the route. You may need a navigator on a bicycle to lead the way. Try to arrange your start from a popular pedestrian area or town centre garden. Raise a tape and use a noisy starting pistol. Borrow a 'Personality' or local politician or senior officer of your charity to start the race and suggest that a local radio station might like to broadcast from the route. Use your VIP to reinforce 'rules' of behaviour and remind the teams that collecting money is the name of the game. Keep tabs on how the race is going. For the 'marathon' version telephone your local radio station several times to let them know how it is progressing.

What happens at the end?

Finish in another popular spot, or arrive back at the start. Try finishing near a bandstand which you could use to hold a winners ceremony. Give each member of the teams a ribbon with a little medal. These are fairly inexpensive and are easily available from trophy shops. Your VIP can present the trophy. You can keep up the momentum by providing music and refreshments: keep collectors collecting until the bitter end!

Individual sponsorship forms need to be signed or marked to indicate that the competitor completed the route, or pushed for so many miles; a table set up just after the finishing line is the best place to organise this. Have at least four officials with rubber stamps to prevent queues forming.

If your runners are running over a long period of time arrange for refreshments or at least a cup of hot soup to be available. At the end of the Norfolk Marathon Campbells Foods donate the soup each year, it is doled out by members of the WRVS from a caravan.

Possible problems?

You might find that your local police have banned bed pushes. Don't argue with them, just choose another fundraising idea that they are happy with, or try another area.

Street Collection permits often need to be applied for up to a year in advance. Officially, open collecting buckets, or barrows, are illegal as collecting tins are supposed to be sealed. In some areas open containers are tolerated and it is obviously much quicker and easier for people to throw money into a bucket than have to feed it into a slot.

Make sure someone is specifically responsible for fulfilling the conditions of the permit and don't forget that collectors have to be 16 or over (18 in London). You will have to make a full financial return by law by an appointed date. It is easy to forget this after the event is over.

A conventional hospital bed may not stand up to the test of a marathon. Consider getting it specially strengthened or swapping it half way along the route. Rubber tyres make a much more comfortable ride, but include a spare wheel and a puncture repair kit.

People can get injured during this sort of event so be prepared for all eventualities.

FUN RUN

Operating requirements: Committee consisting of a co-ordinator, treasurer, secretary, and several other members to assist on the day according to the size of your event. First-aider.

Equipment needs: Suitable venue – marked out park, field, playing field or recreation ground is ideal. Collection tins. Starting and finishing tapes. Public address system or megaphone. Starting pistol. Refreshments. First aid kit.

Lead time: Four to six months.

Initial cost: Very little outlay. Prizes should be sponsored.

Suitable for: Anything and everything.

Expected return: Work on an average of £10 raised by each entrant. Hopefully you should be able to do much better than this. The collection should bring in another £50 – £100 at a small event. If you sell refreshments you can raise more money.

What's in it for contributors: As above, a thoroughly enjoyable, and competitive, event that is as equally fun to watch as to take part. Prizes for different 'classes'.

Frequency: Annually in the same area.

Special requirements: A street collection licence from the Local Authority. You might need to inform the Police.

Variations on a theme: Pram race. Waiters race – individuals have to race over a given route dressed as waiters carrying a metal tray, bottle and two (unbreakable) glasses, as supplied by the organisers. Pancake race for Shrove Tuesday – the Gas Board can set up mobile stoves to cook pancakes on site – individuals run (in fancy dress) carrying frying pans with pancakes, tossing as they go.

How does it work?

Teams or individuals race against each other (or against their own stamina/determination) over an arranged route. You raise money from entry fees, sponsorship, a public collection and refreshments or side stalls. The idea is make the event as silly as possible to attract a large crowd as well as competitors.

You could charge, say, £5 entrance for each team or £2 for an individual which would pay for a trophy for the winners if you wanted to make this an annual event. Persuading the competitors to enter in fancy-dress all helps the event to be more PR-worthy. It is also more of a laugh for all concerned. Prizes can be awarded to the best (and worst!) dressed teams.

How do we get started?

Form an organising group as above and decide on your venue and a date. Fun runs are best held in the mornings; perhaps the middle of July and August are best avoided so that competitors do not suffer from heat exhaustion. If you are to dress up as Fozzy Bear or a Smurf, much better for it to be less than 20 degrees, on the other hand you are unlikely to get much of a turn out if you choose the Easter holidays when it can still be very chilly. School half-terms are notoriously bad dates also due to people taking long weekends away.

If you are planning a large event on a central site look for company sponsorship early on. Your benefiting charity might be experienced in finding sponsorship and might be able to help you here. (See chapter on sponsorship.)

Find a bank or building society that will be prepared to open a paying-in account for you and get your sponsorship forms printed. You will need at least five hundred for a medium scale event and if you have them printed on white or a pale colour (not pink or red) you will be able to photocopy more if you run out.

Try not to have too many rules. Almost anything goes. If people want to enter a team of two, three or even six, let them. If children under 10 want to start half way up the field, why not? It's not a sporting event and your main aim is to make money and have fun so let the event grow organically. Just keep a special eye on safety issues.

Remember to request the St. John Ambulance or the Red Cross to attend, you will need them for minor sprains if nothing more serious. When you plan your site allow an emergency vehicle route, just in case you need to get an ambulance through in a hurry.

You will need toilet facilities, somewhere for people to sit and you should organise a tent or building where runners can have blisters dressed or get cups of tea free of charge. Outside you can have refreshment stalls for spectators where you hope to make a small profit.

You will need to think about car parking and you may need the police to advise you in this area. Whatever you do, make sure that runners and cars are kept well apart.

As in the Bed Push Marathon, make sure that you will be granted a Street Collection Permit for that day. (See chapter on Tax, Licences, Rules and Regulations for details.)

Four weeks before the event make advice sheets and sponsorship forms available from well publicised sources. If you can involve the local radio or newspaper office, their reception areas and that of your sponsoring company all make good pick-up points. You must also have a telephone contact advertised so that people can ring in and be sent a form.

What about publicity?

If you involve the media as suggested above, you are half way there. They will take on a good deal of your advertising requirements for you, but you will still need some good quality posters and leaflets to pass on to as many public buildings, libraries, sports clubs, schools contacts of your charity etc. as you can. Look for competitors as above in hospitals, schools, factories, restaurants and pubs or advertise through the Chamber of Commerce magazine or in-house council workers' news letters.

What happens on the day?

Arrive in good time. People will want to check in up to an hour before the start of the race. They should hand over their forms and be given a corresponding number to pin on. The forms are kept in numerical order so that they can be found quickly as each runner finishes, marked with the number of laps achieved and rubber stamped. Use stewards wearing brightly coloured waistcoats to direct runners to the checking in areas. Checking in should stop within fifteen minutes of the start time to enable the organisers to arrange the forms into the correct order and divide them into batches ready for the finish. See 'Possible problems' at the end of the this section.

Encourage your VIP competitors to mingle with the crowd and start to build up some excitement. Use a compere to organise the competitors and control the crowd, music always adds to the attraction of the event.

Measure your track in advance and mark it out in tenths of a mile. The whole circuit needs to be half or one mile so that you can work out how many miles each runner completes. If your track is any shorter than half a mile then you will start to get stragglers caught up by the front runners and you won't be able to work out how many laps they have completed. Make sure that you have a board clearly visible from the track and the checking in tables showing what lap is being run. Some events use several lap recorders. These people must be responsible and keep 'awake' – there is plenty of room for acrimony at the end if runners feel short-changed.

As runners finish, they can peel off to one side to have their forms stamped and medals given out if you are using them.

As soon as the event is over you can present the prizes to the person or team completing the most laps. Other prizes such as the silliest costume or oldest runner can be given out also. Unless you have a computer on site, and you can provide one easily with the advent of the lap-top, you will have to delay presenting the prize for the person who raised the most amount of money.

Make sure that everyone involved is thanked profusely and that you clear the area of litter and equipment before you leave.

 **HANDY HINT**

Hold a children's Fun Run an hour before the main one gets started and halt it after 45 minutes. This gives tinies a chance to compete but stops you getting your main event snarled up with very slow runners.

What happens after the event?

For two or three weeks your main concern is to retrieve all the pledges. If you operate using the guidelines as outlined at the beginning of this chapter you should be able to bank 80-90% of promised monies.

When you have completed your accounts, organise a 'grand handing-over'. Invite the press, the company sponsors, donors of prizes, your sponsorship winner and anyone else who helped in a big way as

PLUS & MINUS

- ⊞ Great fun and potentially lucrative event.
- ⊞ Needs careful but not prolonged organisational skills.
- ⊞ Shouldn't require large setting up costs.
- ⊞ Very attractive to potential sponsors.
- ⊞ Easy to publicise.
- ⊞ Family event.
- ⊞ Easy to scale up or down according to circumstances.

- ⊟ Needs a lot of volunteer helpers.
- ⊟ Can be chaotic if not organised properly.
- ⊟ Can involve injury, needs professional medical teams available.
- ⊟ Not suitable for very young children.

well as a representative of the cause for whom you were all fundraising. Arrange for some photographs of the giant cheque and the prize being presented to your most successful fundraiser to be taken, in case the newspaper photographer is late or doesn't show up.

If you get the feeling that the event would benefit from another airing make some arrangements to meet after a month or two so that you can discuss organising a similar event for next year.

Possible problems?

As in the Bed Push Marathon, be aware that you might need to apply for permission to hold a public collection up to a year in advance on popular days.

Unless you organise your checking in tables very carefully you are liable to hold-ups which is very undesirable when you have exhausted and possibly injured people waiting for you to find forms and stamp them. Organise four to eight funnels with ropes or crowd control barriers to direct numbered entrants. Each funnel should be marked clearly 1-30, 30-60 or however you chose to separate your runners.

POLE SITTING (and other zany feats)

Operating requirements: One individual and perhaps a sponsorship co-ordinator.

Equipment needs: Custom built pole or a platform in a suitable tree, ideally in a public place. Public address system or megaphone at the start.

Lead time: A few weeks.

Initial cost: Very little outlay, most of the publicity is done through the media. The cost of sponsorship forms. Try to get the pole donated.

Suitable for: Anything and everything.

Expected return: Almost everything received is profit.

What's in it for contributors: I think this one appeals to people because it is so weird and sponsors are glad that it is someone else attempting the record.

Frequency: One-off.

Special requirements: If you plan to pole-sit in a public space you will probably need permission from the local authority.

Variations on a theme: As an individual you can try a 'sponsored-almost-anything'. You only have to choose something that you want to try yourself and that you think will capture the public imagination.

What on earth is pole sitting?

This is a truly bizarre activity which started in America. A specially constructed pole, the taller the better but at least seven feet high, is set firmly into the ground. On top of this telegraph-pole-like structure is usually a barrel or a small shack-like structure.

Sitters sit for days, weeks, even months at a time, apparently without falling off, being fed by volunteers who pass up food and drink at intervals. And... No, I don't know the answers to your other questions! I guess it is all according to the individual. According to the Guinness Book of Records a woman, Mellissa Sanders, lived in a hut 6'x7' on top of a pole in Indianapolis for a total of 516 days. Whew!

Pole-sitting in this country is not a popular occupation and it is certainly not something that I have tried, although Rob Colley stayed in a barrel on top of a pole 43ft high at Dartmouth Wildlife Park for over 42 days, completing his 'sit' on 24 August 1992 (source: Guinness Book of Records). I think most charities have had parachutists, bungee jumpers and bridge swingers, so I am offering the challenge of a UK pole-sitter to come forward and see if you can capture the nation's heart, and money. I should love to hear how you get on.

PLUS & MINUS

- ⊞ It is your idea and you can do just what appeals to you.
- ⊞ You can make the event as high or low-key as you wish.
- ⊞ If you chose a really zany idea you should find it easy to gain media interest.
- ⊞ If you aim to beat a record you will gain extra media coverage.
- ⊞ If you work with a charity you can leave all the actual fundraising to someone else.
- ⊟ Hard work to find your own sponsorship.
- ⊟ Often experimental, but it has its compensations.
- ⊟ Might find local authority resistance.

How shall I get started?

Well, if it were me (which it won't be!) I should start practising on a small pole first. Try a barrel on a tea chest and see if you can cope with several hours without falling off or becoming so cramped you have to get down.

When you are quite good at your chosen occupation contact the media or the Guinness Book of Records and state that you are going to set a UK pole-sitting record.

Having achieved some media interest you could contact BT or a timber company and see if they will supply you with a pole to sit on and erect it for you. BT were extraordinarily helpful with the 'Fire Over England' project in the eighties. Pole-sitting just might be the sort of crazy idea that interests them. Any number of breweries or cider companies should be happy to supply you with a barrel.

What do I do to get a record into the Guinness Book of Records?

You need to put your idea into writing in the form of a brief proposal at least two months before you attempt the record. Write to Peter Mathews, Guinness Publishing Ltd, 33 London Road, Enfield, Middlesex, EN2 6DJ.

How do I go about getting the sponsorship?

Some ideas work best run hand in hand with the benefiting charity. I think this could be one of them. Suggest that you do the sitting and finding the volunteers to look after you and they organise a nation wide sponsorship drive. You could both be on to a very good thing. You for notoriety and the cause for the cash. For a more usual type of individual event you will have to find a sponsorship team yourself.

What about when it is all over?

Well, when you have had enough sitting 'atop your pole or if you fell off when you went to sleep, announce your national (or regional) record and start to collect your sponsorship money. Give yourself and your sponsors about a month to get your total in and then announce your final figure and arrange a hand-over as outlined above.

Your ace is the uniqueness of your idea, so play on it for all its worth, as you would if you had been using an idea that was spectacularly dangerous or impressive. Use the media as much as you can and then set about breaking your own record.

EVENT 22 STREET COLLECTION OR FLAG DAY

Collecting donations from the public in the street

Operating requirements: Representative of bone fide charitable or benevolent organisation. As many collectors, over 16, as you can muster.

Equipment needs: Collecting boxes or tins. Flags or stickers if required.

Lead time: 3–6 months.

Initial cost: Nothing or very little if you are using stickers. The charity for whom you are collecting may supply their own.

Suitable for: All types of fundraising. City centres, parks, at other events, open air meetings, arcades, stations, cinemas, pubs, theatres or even the frontage of shops and stores.

Expected return: How long is a piece of string? Seriously, the more collectors you use, the more cash they will collect.

What's in it for contributors: Nothing, bar the warm glow of a happy conscience! But people still give.

Frequency: As often as you like on private property. You may be restricted to just a few times a year on that deemed to be 'a public place'.

Special requirements: To hold a collection in a public place (not necessarily the same as public property) you will need a street collection permit.

How does it work?

You do nothing other than ask people to give you money for a particular cause. Sometimes they will and sometimes they won't but you can't follow people around or coerce them. You need to display the name of your charity clearly.

There are ways in which you can dress the collection up to entertain, educate or appeal to potential donors.

Will I need to apply for a Street Collection Permit?

The Local Government Act, 1972 gives powers to Local Authorities to regulate collections on public property. The Charities Act, 1992 tightened these regulations further (see below) and you will be required to comply with this legislation whenever you hold a collection on any street or public place. Whilst shopping precincts may be deemed to be a public place, cinemas, theatres, railway stations, steps of churches or

HANDY HINT

Invite all your collectors to an official hand-over of the final total. Ask the bank to prepare a giant cheque and take a photograph of everyone holding it. People do like to feel appreciated and it also provides a good PR opportunity for your cause.

within the boundaries of a shop are private, at least for the present (Feb 1994). The legislation described above will be replaced shortly by Part III of the Charities Act 1992 (Sections 65-74) regulating what will become known as 'Public Charitable Collections'. As yet the new regulations have not been published but the definition 'public place' will be extended to definitely include shopping precincts, shop frontages, highways and railway stations later in 1994. Offices, hospitals and schools will be exempt as will any place to which a ticket must be purchased to gain access.

Although requirements vary slightly around the country, broadly the basis on which a permit is granted is very much the same and this is unlikely to change.

You are required to apply, in writing, to the Administration Department of the district council covering the area where you intend to hold the collection, at least one month prior to the event. In practice you may have to apply well before that to ensure you book the date you need. Be warned that there is much competition for Saturdays and the weeks approaching Christmas.

There are rules that apply and you must adhere to them. (See the chapter on Rules and Regulations for details.) You should also be aware that all your collectors must be over 16 (over 18 in London), carry a written authority from the promoter and wear badges. You will also be required to complete a return slip giving the Council information including the total amount collected, who counted it and a list of all the collectors.

Where the new regulations may show significant changes is covering matters relating to the keeping and publishing of accounts, preventing annoyance and carrying certificates, so make yourselves aware of developments by contacting your local authority.

Where might I collect without a permit?

Assuming that you have requested and obtained permission from the owners, you may collect anywhere on private property as outlined above. However, where, before the new regulations, you were allowed to hold a collection at an open air meeting or an event on public land, you now will have to obtain a permit unless you are selling tickets to that event. In short, most events that charge an entry fee will be exempt. However, areas of private land to which the public have general access will be seen as a 'public place' in the eyes of the law.

Some of the places that successful collections have been held include private houses; pubs; trains; railway, bus and underground stations (no longer exempt from 1994); inside shops and stores, (the pavement outside will not be exempt in 1994); after the show in a cinema or theatre; as part of an event on a private field or in a garden; and, of course, every Sunday in churches all over the country. Interestingly if someone lives in a pub (and most of them are residentially occupied) a collection, especially a pub-to-pub collection, might be liable for a house-to-house collection licence, although I have not heard of any such enforcement.

How do I obtain the collecting boxes?

If you contact the benefiting charity's headquarters to explain your plans, and you should do so to get their approval for your idea, they will advise you. Stickers or flags may be made available, record sheets and seals will certainly be so.

Officially, the tins or boxes need to be closed and sealed and this is good practice as it assures the donor that the money will go where it is intended. Each box should be numbered. All boxes should be opened in the presence of two people, with the contents of each box counted, checked and recorded as soon after the collection as possible.

Occasionally you might be able to use buckets or other open topped collecting tubs, especially for a fun run, street procession or sponsored walk. In this case all the collection buckets will have to bear an official sticker and collectors must still be over 16. Buckets should be emptied at a supervised central collection point and directly the event has ended monies should be removed to a secure place for counting to take place. Be warned that counting can take hours! At the end of the Lord Mayor's Street Procession in Norwich in excess of several thousand pounds in small change is regularly collected during the space of an evening. Counting the proceeds is a mammoth task and involves experienced volunteers from the Treasury Department using special coin weighing machines; and it still takes most of the night.

PLUS & MINUS

- ⊞ No need to hire a venue.
- ⊞ Very little organisation required.
- ⊞ Works well with another event.
- ⊞ No outlay.
- ⊟ May need permit.
- ⊟ May not be able to collect on the day you want.
- ⊟ Not suitable for children under 16.

How can we make our flag day more exciting?

Try putting all the collectors in fancy dress. This is particularly good if you are fundraising for an animal charity. Remember, though, that some people feel intimidated or frightened by people in fancy dress so make it appropriate and leave some collectors in regular clothing.

For a charity that is, perhaps, less popular or well known, ask for permission to mount a small mobile exhibition alongside the collectors explaining your cause and handing out leaflets to those who show an interest or run a collection 50:50 with a more popular organisation.

Try running your collection alongside another event, although you will have to choose carefully as there will be some competition unless the event is for the same cause.

Get permission to play music, borrow a barrel-organ or perform some circus acts to grab the passer-by's attention. (Don't forget that if your flag day turns into a musical event you may have to apply for a Public Entertainment Licence, see back of the book for details.)

Think up some zany ideas. Collect from horseback or use some other old fashioned means of transport.

Use strange collecting boxes, if you are allowed, such as policemen's helmets when collecting at the Police Gala Day, Wellington boots for the Gardener's Benevolent Fund or bedpans for the hospital.

EVENT 23

SPINE-CHILLER TRAIL

Guided ghostly walk

Operating requirements: Co-ordinator/guide, treasurer.

Equipment needs: Strong, clear voice that will stand the course, torch.

Lead time: Two weeks minimum , but allow yourselves enough time to advertise.

Initial cost: Just publicity costs.

Suitable for: Local appeals and charities. Needs to be in a well populated tourist area.

Expected return: £40 maximum, each trail.

What's in it for contributors: An interesting and creepy, guided tour.

Frequency: Every Sunday from March to October providing you are not under threat from commercial or official Tourist Board competition.

Special requirements: Thorough knowledge of your local area and its history. You may need access to buildings and permission to poke about the grounds of others.

Variations on a theme: Apart from a general guided tour, what about an architects trail, or a bridges tour in London, a riverside walk, or an owl trail in the countryside. How about an early morning river trip if you know someone who would lend a cruiser or an electric boat, or a brass-rubbing tour in the city. Heritage tours are often popular as are, unaccountably, guided trips of the sewers!

How does it work?

A group of up to twenty people pay about £2.00 each to be told ghostly tales and led into spooky places for about an hour and a half.

How do I get started?

Perhaps you are interested in this idea because you know some tales about the area in which you live. Gather as much information as you can about a couple of square miles and explore any churches, ruins, graveyards, old houses, woods or cliffs that might have appropriate legends associated with them. Reject the temptation to make things up, but do dress up historical facts by learning to paint verbal pictures and making suggestions as to what may have happened to arrive at a particular event. Use the library or local historians to direct you. Aim to be able to talk about everything without having to refer to notes.

Devise a route to cover as many interesting places as you can without covering the same ground twice. You should hope to be back where you started, or at a friendly pub, within about an hour or an hour and a half.

This includes stops where you will talk. It might be a good idea to arrange your start and finish by a cathedral or in a hotel where people can congregate without getting too wet or cold before you set off.

Make sure that you get permission from all the appropriate authorities to traipse around their property or through their gardens. Where you can, obtain access to the inside of churches, up towers or sites of grim happenings but don't plan more than three or four of these explorations or you will restrict the time you can spend looking at other things.

HANDY HINT

Above all, be professional. Go on a few other trails to see how they are done.

Should I arrange more than one trail?

You won't need to devise more than one route, but you do need to run it fairly often if you are going to make any money from the idea.

Your publicity will take up all you make from the first trail, but it won't cost you any more to market twenty trails than if you were just selling a one-off.

So how do I market it?

Decide on all the dates you will run the trail, then advertise the whole list. Print some A5 leaflets to describe the evening. Publish the price, the dates and the time and place you start from. Give a 'phone number to ring so walkers can book, but leave payment until the night, in cash.

Let the local Tourist Information Centre know of your plans fairly early on. They will be able to advise if you have competition and may be able to take bookings for you. They will certainly add your trails to their list of events. Send press releases to the local media and an invitation to a couple of journalists and a photographer to join the group for the first one. Consider advertising in the What's On column of the local paper if it is not too expensive. They may do a free entry if they know it is for charity.

How do I organise the trail on the night?

Arrive about ten minutes before the set off time; about 8.30pm is about right. You may need to make it later in the Summer as it will still be light until 9.00pm. Try not to have more than twenty people on one trail or it will be difficult to keep everyone together and they may not all be able to hear you, especially if it is windy.

Start on time and always keep to your planned route and talk. You will have to be very experienced before you can extemporise successfully.

You will save yourself a big worry if you ensure that at least one other person knows the spiel and the route as well as you. If you are stuck visiting Great Aunt Nora, or the dog has to be rushed to the vet or you just fancy a Sunday to yourself you will feel happier knowing that there is a stand-in.

Give people an idea of how long the walk will take and let them know where you plan to finish if it is not where you started. Ask for questions and when everyone is happy with what is about to happen, collect the

PLUS & MINUS

- + Very little outlay.
- + No venue to hire and no infrastructure.
- + Only needs a couple of people to set up and just one guide each evening.
- + Good for families though probably best to suggest over 7s only.

- − Needs careful planning and you might need to obtain several permissions.
- − Best in well populated tourist area.
- − May have commercial competition. In York, for instance, guides and their audiences are falling over each other at every popular monument.

money so that people can drift away later if they are cold or tired (not bored, of course) and you don't lose out.

Arrive at your final destination punctually, spend some time answering any more questions and give people a little one-to-one attention. This helps your customers feel they have had value for money but gives those who want to an opportunity to go home.

Afterwards, put your feet up, get yourself a drink and have a rest. You will have earned it!

EVENT 24 STALLS AND SIDESHOWS

Many events rely on stalls and stands to provide interest and colour and they can be a great source of revenue. The WI have got so good at running stalls that they now have a commercial operation called WI Markets doing nothing else but holding regular sales from stalls of produce and goods. Village fayres, church fetes and other fundraising days often consist of little else. And so long as the variety and quality of activities and items offered for sale are well considered, visitors will feel they have had an enjoyable afternoon out. It is, after all, the backbone of English country summer activities.

However, a motley collection of doors on trestles selling junk that is only worth putting in the bin or a stall offering insect covered, tired looking cakes or a tombola comprised of out-of-date cans of beans and tinned tomatoes that would do justice to the compost heap, all dotted about over a windy field, is not going to inspire anyone to part with their money or come again another time.

In this chapter I hope to encourage you to design and prepare your stalls attractively, we will look at how grouping them correctly can make all the difference to your proceeds and finally I shall give you loads of good, and proven, ideas.

How do I make a stall?

The door over two trestles, as described above, is not such a bad idea in itself. But you do need to pretty it up in some way. Sheets, tablecloths and non-rip crepe paper secured firmly with drawing pins are all ideal. If you are running a stall regularly you might consider dyeing a sheet or two a darker colour to provide a more colourful background.

Suit your colours and surfaces to your produce. It is pretty obvious really; green or brown for vegetables, a bright tablecloth for cakes, Hessian or bare wood for plants, pink or powder blue for baby clothes, black or red for shoes etc. This all helps to give your stall an identity of its own and helps customers subconsciously gravitate towards the kind of products that they are particularly interested in.

You might be able to borrow some trestle tables from the local community centre, school or church hall. These are ideal as a longer than average table length is required for most stalls. Remember, however, that if you damage them you will have to pay and they may not be so helpful next time – use picnic cloth spring clips for holding on cloths instead of pins and nails. In extremis you can hire tables from marquee firms or some tool hire companies.

For a more sophisticated appearance try hanging a banner or flags flying between two seven foot poles nailed or tied firmly onto each end of the table or pushed into the ground. For a bottle stall or a stand selling

> **HANDY HINT**
>
> To give an incentive to stall holders to make their stalls look good run a competition for the 'best-dressed stall'. Ask a VIP to judge and present some rosettes towards the end of the afternoon.

lots of small items use risers (small blocks or shelves) to display your products to advantage, this can help a small display look more substantial especially as stock gets low towards the end of the day. Make risers from bricks or weighted boxes covered in wallpaper or cloth. Use velcro to stick packaged samples to a back board. Some stalls look better with a background and the sales person selling from the front. Embroidery, jewellery or other delicate items are enhanced by this treatment.

Remember to provide yourself and your helpers (at least two per stall) with something to sit on. Standing for four or more hours is tiring and you will know all about it the next day. You will also need a float of money and something to put it in. A couple of plastic boxes, one inside the other, will do. Put notes in the bottom box and they will not blow away or be obvious prey to the opportunist thief.

Pack an emergency bag the night before your event and include scissors, paper, pens, drawing pins, a staple gun, sticky tape, safety pins and dress maker's pins (as appropriate) so you can make extra price labels if necessary. A couple of large round stones are often useful as paperweights. You might need a large piece of card to give your stall a title, such as Tombola, White Elephant, Guess the Weight of the Cake, etc. so that customers can see from a distance what you are providing. Include some plasters, sting relief cream or midge repellent if you are outside. Even a hat or coat can be very welcome if you are stuck behind a stall for hours at a time in hot sun or a keen wind. Remember, also, to make provision for refreshments for the helpers. Usually you will be able to get the odd cup of tea on site but you will be very popular with your neighbours if you pack a flask and a couple of mugs!

Make sure someone will be bringing a basic tool kit and a hammer and nails; if you are not certain, pack these too. I have never known an event yet that didn't need some kind of major repair made or some ingenious device erected just before opening time.

Where do I put my stall?

The most well organised fetes plan their site well in advance and erect a site plan at the entrance so that stall holders and visitors can see at a glance where everything is.

Sometimes you walk onto a site and know immediately who the co-ordinator is, not because s/he is clasping a clip board or sitting behind a desk in the secretary's tent, but because they are running about all over the area trailing a tail of worried looking people, all of whom are trying to get their questions answered. This should be avoided at all costs!

At a big show stall holders should be given the number of their pitch in advance and the site laid out carefully to allow vehicles behind each row. They will be able drive straight onto the site, find their pitch and unload their products all without bothering anyone.

If it is you who is arranging where all the stalls should go there are some basic rules to follow, the most important being to keep your stalls close together and tightly packed. Just because Farmer Jones has lent you a fifty acre meadow doesn't mean that you have to use it all. It is much more attractive to have a busy, exciting corner than a whole field covered in lonely little stands that need a Sherpa to guide you round to the next one.

Take some tips from the big stores and supermarkets. Put a few bright, popular stands near the entrance to encourage people through the gate. A Fruit Raffle or Preserve Stall might be good. Then come the store-cupboard basics such as Fishing for Ducks, Steady Hand Driving or a Hoopla. You might see some speciality products next, appealing to a more specific market. These could include more vigorous activities which keep the men happy such as a Coconut Shy, Bowling for the Pig, Catch the Rat or Aunt Sally. You can develop a noisy, fairground area which you can follow on with a different group of stalls appealing to another type of customer, perhaps craft stands and handmade clothes. Do you see the idea? Keep the site in bunches of like with like, similar to a department store. People enjoy one activity and look around to repeat the experience immediately. If they don't like what they see they can move swiftly through that 'department' until they come to an area in which they feel more comfortable.

Save the refreshments to the end of the site. Encourage your visitors to walk past every available activity before you allow them to sit down and enjoy a cup of tea. The cake stalls go here too. Imagine resting your weary feet and tucking into the most delicious chocolate cake with some home-made lemonade. You lean back in your chair to enjoy the sunshine and your eyes rest on a table full of glorious cakes for sale. Would you be able resist buying one or two to take back home? The same goes for strawberry teas. Arrange to sell extra punnets of strawberries and raspberries next to where the teas are served.

If you have a car park, plan an outpost from your fete and sell your garden produce – flowers, vegetables and plants from here. Customers are more likely to buy these bulky and often heavy items if they can put them straight into their cars.

Where stalls are just part of a larger event arrange your selling area around the outside of an arena or at least confined to one area. Keep children's activities near the refreshments so that Mums and Dads can sit down whilst keeping an eye on little Tommy. You will sell extra cups of tea and especially the odd beer or two if the children are occupied. But remember that children must not be allowed in licensed areas.

It is kinder, but not such good business sense I agree, to keep sweet stands and candy floss away from the children's activities. I get really irritated when I am forced to buy sweets for my children to stop them from ruining a day out because the organisers have stuck temptation right under their noses. My opinion is that parents should be allowed to make their own decisions and I have actually gone home early because an event has been so overbalanced with sweets and junk food. The same goes for too many collectors rattling tins under your nose at every corner, however good the cause. The secret is to keep a good variety and moderation in everything.

...And now for the ideas.

LUCKY NUMBER

Equipment needs:

- An easel or table secured firmly on a slight slope rather like a designer's drawing board.
- A large sheet of paper or card marked out into numbered squares about 5 x 5cm large. Write the numbers in the upper half of the square only and leave the lower half blank. Or write them large but in a pale crayon so that you can write over.
- Biro and float.
- Prize or prizes.

How it works

This is a game of chance. Agree with a colleague which number is the 'Lucky Number' and make a note of it. Players pay for each chance. They choose a number and write their name (and 'phone number if they are not planning to stay to the end) in the square. The winner is the person who wrote his or her name in the pre-agreed numbered square. Obviously the bigger the card, the more squares you can have available and the larger the proceeds.

GUESS THE NUMBER OF SWEETS

Equipment needs:

- Large clear jar.
- Known amount of sweets.
- Record pad and biro.
- Prize (which may be the sweets themselves) or cash.

How it works

This game is classified as a game of skill. It is very flexible as you can walk around with the jar or have a stall. You can adjust your product to suit the occasion, for instance at a Model Makers Exhibition you could fill your jar with nuts and bolts.

Your player makes a guess as to the quantity in the jar and you record their name and telephone number on the pad. The winner is the contestant who comes nearest to guessing the correct figure. In the case of more than one correct answer, the first guess is the winner.

GUESS THE WEIGHT OF THE CAKE

Equipment needs:

- Large cake wrapped tightly in greaseproof paper (a fruit cake is best).
- Record pad and biro

How it works

This is a popular variation of the Guess the Sweets. Remember to wrap the cake carefully because people will want to handle it. In this case the prize is the cake and the game works as above. Other variations can include: Guess the weight of the baby or the dog or anything else you care to think of.

DOOR KEYS

Equipment needs:

- A clear fronted box with a Yale lock and two keys.
- A large box filled with as many Yale keys as you can get hold of.
- Prize that fits in the box.

How it works

Charge 5p or 10p for a chance to pick a key and try the lock. The one who opens the box wins the prize. Those who are unlucky replace the key into the box for others to try their luck. The more keys you have the harder it is. Keep a spare key out so that you can open the box!

LUCKY DIP OR BRAN TUB

Equipment needs:

- Tub or barrel half full of bran, sawdust or straw. (For a particularly revolting variation of this game you can mix the bran with water, wrap the prizes in plastic bags and have a SLIME DIP! Don't use wallpaper paste as they frequently have toxic fungicides added.)
- Selection of small prizes.
- Wrapping paper (could be newspaper) and tape.

How it works

Everyone has played this game at some stage or another, but it is often a disappointment, both in terms of how much money is made and the suitability of the prizes. Very simply, you pay your money and have one dip into the bran tub. Whatever is retrieved is kept.

A slightly mean, but more profitable, variation on the original – remember everyone wins a prize – is as follows:

First, to ensure that prizes are suitable, arrange two tubs. These are separated into 3 yrs and under and 4 yrs and over or boys and girls (with a proviso that under 36 months is not recommended – you have to be very careful about toys for small children). Then comes the mean bit; put presents in two thirds of the boxes but leave one third empty, wrap them all up and bury them as usual. Make sure that your display indicates that you might not win anything such as 'Try your luck at winning a prize'.

Fix your charge carefully. Add together the value of all the prizes including wrapping, bran and tubs if you hired them, double it, then divide by the number of prizes. You will make double your money on each prize plus what you make on the empty prizes.

There are commercial companies who provide egg shaped capsules containing prizes. Contacts are at the back of the book.

CATCH THE RAT

Equipment needs:

- Long, substantial tube. A 5 ft length of guttering downpipe would do well.
- Wood and gutter brackets.
- Long handled mallet or croquet mallet (but it must be pretty beefy as it will come in for some punishment).
- Wooden ball or supply of plastic balls of a diameter to roll down the tube easily.
- Grass paint (whitewash) such as is used on sports pitches.

How to make your rat launcher

Fix the tube to a framework of wood using the gutter brackets allowing a 60 degree angle to the ground. The tube should leave a space between the end and the ground twice the diameter of the ball. The tube should be open at both ends. Paint an eighteen inch diameter circle on the ground in front of the end of the tube. You can experiment to find the optimum place, depending on the degree of difficulty. Paint a rat's face on your ball, for added authenticity.

How it works

There is one attempt per charge or three for a discount. The 'catcher' grasps the mallet, looks at the circle and says go (or not if you wish to make it harder!). The operator releases the 'rat' at the top of the tube and the punter has to try to smash it before it leaves the circle when it appears at the bottom.

This looks so easy but it is really difficult to hit the rat in the circle. You need superhuman powers of concentration and reflexes. Those of us, and we all know someone, who will not be beaten try again and again and still come back for more serious humiliation!

Variation:

Instead of using a ball you can use a bean bag with a painted face, string tail and ears to look like a rat. Fix your downpipe to the base board but leave 18" of wood below the opening. The 'catcher' has to thwack the rat against the board, using a baseball bat or similar, before it hits the ground.

FISHING FOR DUCKS

Equipment needs:

- 10 ducks carved from balsa wood, the bill is given a slight hook downwards, and painted.
- 20 x 6 inch nails.
- 2 x 'Fishing lines' made from bamboo, light string with a small brass ring instead of a hook. This must be able to fit over the duck's bills. One is a spare.
- Large tin bath, half filled with water.
- Waterproof felt pen.
- Stop watch.
- Prize or cash prize. (As this is a game of skill you are not restricted to non-cash prizes.)

How to make your ducks

Hammer two nails into the bottom of each duck to resemble legs. This will keep them upright in the water and provide some stability when being hooked. Write numbers, one to ten on the base of each duck.

How it works

Each 'fisherman' pays a fee for a designated length of time fishing. You will have to adjust the time according to how easy your ducks are to hook. Usually it is between thirty and sixty seconds.

Using tremendous skill, your customer must stand upright and holding the bottom end of the rod try to place the ring over the duck's bill. Having done this they then have to lift the duck completely out of the bath. They then try for another duck again and again until the time runs out.

The operator counts up the numbers displayed on each duck caught. Anyone reaching a score of 35 or more wins their money back or has a free go. These contestants have their names recorded and the highest score of the day wins a prize.

There are commercial Hook-a-Duck games that you can hire; see the back of the book for contacts.

TREASURE ISLAND

Equipment needs:

- Map of the treasure island. This can be as elaborate as you like. If you plan to use this idea regularly you could try making a relief map from oasis covered with fabric and painted. Otherwise a creative piece of art work attached to a pin-board is all that is needed. The easiest map of all is a map of your area and the treasure is positioned by co-ordinates. The nearest wins.
- A supply of 'flags' made from paper glued around long dressmakers' pins.
- Prize or cash.

How it works

This is a game of skill particularly if you include some very subtle clues. The contestant selects a spot on the map where she thinks the treasure might be buried (or sunk) and plants a flag marked with her name and telephone number. The winner is the flag coming closest to the prearranged 'x marks the spot'. In the case of a flat map you could actually mark the X on the reverse of the map or, for a more dramatic effect (especially if your event is indoors) you could write it on the map in security ink and borrow an ultra violet light to make it visible at the end of the day. Usually the correct answer is placed in a sealed envelope and pinned to the board to be opened at the end of the day in front of everyone.

BALL-IN-A-BUCKET

Equipment needs:

- Plywood sheet at least 18 inches tall by 3 feet wide.
- A length of 4 x 2 wood.
- Hammer and nails.
- Paint.
- Two plastic buckets, or large flower pots.
- 8 tennis balls.
- Grass paint or tape and pegs.
- Prizes.

How to make your bucket catcher

Cut two holes in the plywood so that the buckets fall through and rest tightly on their rims without going right through. Make struts to support the frame at a slight angle to the ground without pushing the buckets back through their holes. Paint a bright colour and display the instructions.

Peg the tape or paint a throwing line on the ground ten or twelve feet from the buckets. You could have a children's line three feet from the buckets.

How it works

For one charge, the player receives four tennis balls which he tries to throw into one of the buckets whilst standing behind the line; if two stay in s/he wins a prize. You can expect two players about every two or three minutes with this popular game but you need to have prizes that are under a pound each to make it pay. Some people become quite skilled.

COCONUT SHY

Equipment needs:

- Traditionally seven coconut rings or pegs are used.
- 30 wooden balls.
- Strong netting and poles to make a safety net.
- A supply of coconuts

How it works

Set your metal pegs firmly into the ground about two feet apart. Erect a safety net behind and to the sides of the throwing area. It will need to be at least seven or eight feet high to be safe. Arrange your coconuts on the top of the pegs.

Players are given four balls each to throw. The object is to dislodge a coconut off its peg onto the ground, thereby winning the coconut.

It is very hard to knock a coconut off so make sure that you don't buy too many coconuts. Reckon on losing one coconut about every ten minutes, less if you are not busy.

There are companies that rent or sell coconut shies; contacts are in the back of the book.

KNOCK 'EM OFF

Equipment needs:

- Self supporting shelf or table about ten feet long and five foot off the ground.
- 30 empty tins, painted in bright colours.
- 20 bean bags.
- Throwing line or tape.
- Backing board or catch net.

How it works

Set your shelf up and arrange the backdrop. Stand the cans in pyramids of six cans each. The player has four bean bags with which he tries to knock a complete pyramid off the shelf whilst standing behind a throwing line. Prizes should be kept to under a pound.

AUNT SALLY

Equipment needs:

- A wooden board painted and cut to resemble a face with a hole for an open mouth, just a squeak larger than the ball or bean bag.
- 4 tennis balls or bean bags or if you want to appeal to the dubious end of the market try wet sponges.
- Throwing tape or grass paint

How it works

This game is very like Ball-in-a-bucket. It was my favourite game at school fetes as we had an Aunt Sally painted to look like the headmistress. If you do the same for your school events I can guarantee your sideshow's queues will be the longest. The object of the game is to get two balls or bean bags through the mouth. Keep your prizes under a pound each.

BOTTLE FISHING

Equipment needs:

- 6 fishing rods as in Fishing for Ducks. The curtain rings must be about one inch in diameter.
- A supply of bottles of soft drinks.
- Round table.
- Whistle or bell.

How it works

This game is a race, there is a prize for every winner. Use about twenty bottles at a time and space them out all over the table. Six players circle the table and at the sound of the whistle or bell they start to 'fish' for a bottle. The object is to drop the curtain ring over the top of the bottle so that it rests flat on the neck. It is surprisingly difficult to achieve.

As soon as a contestant rings a bottle the operator sounds the bell and stops the game. The winner keeps the bottle.

Some bottle tops are just too big to accept the ring and the skill lies in judging which is suitable.

HOOPLA

Equipment needs:

- Round table.
- 20 x 6 inch wooden or plastic rings.
- 20 wooden blocks (the size depends if you want players to ring the block as well as the prize.)
- Supply of prizes. Bags of home-made sweets are often popular, soft drinks, toys, coins etc.
- Tape or grass paint for a throwing line.

How it works

Arrange your prizes on top of each block and space the blocks carefully all over the table.

Players are given three rings with which to try to ring a prize whilst standing behind a throwing line. Some operators insist that the block is ringed also, but most people feel that to ring the prize conclusively is enough. You might want to have a supply of larger rings for small children to use.

WELLY THROWING

Equipment needs:

- A line painted on the grass and a clear space.
- Some Wellington boots.
- Some flags or markers.
- A very long tape measure.
- Something to record the names and throws.
- 2 or 3 prizes.

How it works

Just invite people to pay for the chance to throw a welly as far as they can. This is not as easy as it sounds! Watch out for those who throw backwards instead of forwards! Record how far people throw and give a prize to the furthest throws at the end of the day.

BOWLING FOR THE PIG

Equipment needs:

- Enough stop netting or canvas to line the bowling lane.
- 9 wooden skittles.
- 3 wooden bowling balls.
- A prize. Traditionally a live pig. But you could get a side of ready butchered, frozen pork donated or supply another substantial prize.

How it works

This is a game of challenge. There is only one winner at the end of the day but because the recently vanquished always want a turn to win again, the game is self perpetuating and you take money on every turn.

A player has three balls with which to knock down all nine skittles. If he achieves a strike he may be challenged and if the new player has a strike he in turn may be challenged. If the new player doesn't manage to knock all the skittles over the original player remains the winner until he is challenged and vanquished.

The winner is the latest person to knock all nine skittles down at the end of the day. Play tends to pick up well at the end so you may have to display a finishing time.

PICK A STRAW

Equipment needs:

- 100 wide drinking straws.
- Large tray of sand.
- Raffle tickets.
- Selection of small prizes.

How it works

This idea works on the same principle as the bottle stall; you pay for a chance to win.

Roll up the raffle tickets and poke them into the straws. Stand the straws in the tray of sand. As with the bottle stall, if you reserve tickets that end in 5 or 0 for the prizes it makes finding them a whole lot easier. You could add another variation by including a free turn for any ticket ending in a 3.

MATCHBOX HOUSE

Equipment needs:

- As many empty matchboxes as you can collect.
- Small brass paperclips – the old fashioned sort with two legs that poke through a hole in the paper and open out at the back.
- Glue and sticky-backed plastic (this always reminds me of Blue Peter!)
- Coloured paper or Fablon
- A sheet of plywood

How to make your house

Glue all the matchboxes together to form a large 'chest of drawers'. This is best made with large-size matchboxes. Get all your friends to buy and collect boxes of the same make. You will need at least a hundred boxes, more if you can manage it. You should have a single thickness of boxes, several high and several wide, where all the trays can slide back and forth.

Take all the trays out and poke an old fashioned paperclip through one end of each tray to make a handle. If you cannot buy the clips, a little knot of ribbon will do just as well.

Cover the edges, back and top of the 'chest' with coloured paper, glue it firmly in place and cover with the sticky-backed plastic or you could use Fablon, then stick the plywood onto the back. The wood is not strictly necessary but makes for a much firmer structure and, if you allow it to stand proud of the top, gives you a neat area to paint a roof and display any message you might want such as the price or how much you can win.

Now replace all the trays and you should have a pile of boxes with sliders that can be pulled out forwards by the handles but cannot be pushed through to the back.

WARNING! This game is not strictly legal as detailed at the end of the chapter, but you might like to adapt it so that you feel happy using it. There is something very appealing about matchboxes and children might like playing the game for small items instead of cash.

How it works

This is a game of chance. Put coins into some of the boxes and leave at least half empty. Use about 5 one pound coins and increasing numbers of smaller denomination coins.

Customers pay for each turn (or you could have five for a pound or whatever). They are then allowed to pull out a tray and keep the coin that they may or may not find inside.

This game is particularly good as, if you budget properly, you can never make a loss and you can continuously replenish your boxes, though not too often and in strict secrecy, so that your game never runs out.

SCRATCH CARDS

Equipment needs:

- Collection of scratch cards.
- Cash prizes.

How it works

Customers buy a card and follow instructions printed on the cards by scratching off a variety of silver panels. If the customer reveals a particular combination or specific figure, symbol etc. they win a prize.

Prizes are either given out on the spot or they have to write to the game company for them, depending on the type of card.

Where to get the cards

There are a variety of companies that devise the games and print the cards. You know in advance how much money you will make for your charity, providing you sell all your cards. (Contacts are listed at the back of the book.)

Some games arrive with the prize cards separated from the dud cards. It is intended that the operator feeds them into the game at intervals to make the game more attractive. In my opinion this is wide open to abuse and accusation. Unscrupulous operators have been known to withhold all the big prize cards so that they do not have to pay out at all. One very unfortunate fundraiser reported to me that she knew of an even crueller trick. At large events it is not unusual to find that more than one of these scratch card games are in action. Allegedly the operator of one game bought a ticket for another on the same site and as he did so, using sleight of hand, he slipped all his prize cards into the rival box. So be warned.

Other games arrive with all the cards ready shuffled; this seems to me to be a much fairer way of running the game, although there are those who wish that they knew which box held the big prize cards. It would help not to have the main prizes won in the first ten minutes of any event, which can, and does, happen.

Finally, you must remember that you will have to go to every event with a large amount of cash ready to pay out in prizes if necessary. You might choose to use cheques for better security but you need to know that your bank balance is healthy. If you do not manage to sell all your cards you could be quite seriously out of pocket, what with the cost of the game in the first place (anything between £40 and £100) and the prizes.

However, for all these warnings, the games do work, are popular and I know several experienced fundraisers who use them regularly because they get results.

PRODUCE AND FOOD STALLS

Over the last few years legislation has been tightened considerably over what may or may not be sold in the way of foodstuffs. Many people think that because their event is very small, not for profit or 'only' for charity or that because food is given away and not sold that the law does not apply to them. If only that were true. But unfortunately the bacteria that cause food poisoning are no judge of charity and salmonella contracted at a community barbecue can be just as fatal as when contracted in a large restaurant.

However, since the Food Safety Act 1990 was published there have been a few changes and these will affect charitable organisations. In the main legislation is now less prescriptive and the emphasis has been shifted to identify potential risks as a matter of priority and to look at specific contravention as a secondary and less important role. Inspection 'ratings' have also been changed and village halls, community centres and the like have a lower priority for inspection under the new code, which should make running occasional events a little less worrying. There is also the 'due diligence' defence which has had an important precedent set. Briefly if you are found to contravene the law but that you can show that you acted in a sensible and responsible way and that all reasonable precautions were taken the Courts are likely to take a realistic approach.

It is probably true to say that the local authority is less likely to prosecute, in the event of a serious contravention, quite so severely at a charity event than if you were a multi-million pound burger conglomerate, especially if it can see that you have tried to behave in a responsible manner. But you must make yourselves aware of the Food Safety Act and check where it applies to you and your event. If you use your own kitchen regularly to cook produce for stalls you may have to have your premises registered and inspected. You will find most of what you need to know in 'Organising Local Events' published by Directory of Social Change. Your district Environmental Health Officer should be able to advise you on specific details for your event.

In general, tea, coffee, squash or drinks sold in bottles or cans, jams, pickles and uncooked fruit are all exempt, as are wrapped biscuits, crisps and sweets, bread and cakes that do not contain fresh cream. Areas where you must be especially careful are products containing the following:

- ice cream,
- dairy products,
- meat and cooked meat,
- fish and shell fish,
- pastries or cakes containing fresh cream,
- egg dishes,
- cooked rice or other pulses

This is not a definitive list and care should be taken when preparing or selling all food.

If you have set your heart on having food or home-made produce available, and it is a poor event that is all food for the soul and none for the stomach, then adapt the contents of the chapters concerning Cream Teas and Barbecues to fit the size and style of your own event.

Consider theming your stall, either to suit the event, or to suit yourselves. A Victorian Cake Stall, with everyone dressed in Victorian clothes makes a very pretty scene, or medieval costumes for a Hog-Roast.

OTHER SALES STALLS

Whether your stall is selling books, records, Christmas goods, pottery, cards and stationery, dried flowers or handmade quilts you still need to have some sort of pricing system and probably a record of what you have sold during the event. And you need to have thought it through before you arrive at the fete.

As with the supermarket analogy at the beginning of this chapter, spend some time looking at professional retail shops to discover which lines sell well, make a note of display ideas or whether you should be introducing special offers.

Books and records

Books and records are best sold from cardboard boxes or bread crates. Keep them loosely packed so that customers can flick through without muddling everything up. It is often a good idea to divide your boxes according to price rather than subject or genre unless you are a specialist, the exception being children's books which should be kept separate. Don't forget to have a couple of boxes with books at 5p-10p each. Place one at either end of your stall to encourage people to move nearer and browse. These are equivalent to the dump bins that you see placed near entrances of big stores in the high street.

Quilts, lace and dried flowers

Delicate fabrics or dried flowers are best kept indoors as wind can do a lot of damage in a very short time. Use the display techniques as described at the beginning of the chapter and consider pinning down samples so that you keep the rest of your stock clean.

If you have a local lace-making club, suggest that they bring some unfinished work and provide a demonstration in front of a handicraft stall. You don't have to restrict your sales to lace but it makes a good focal point for the customers. You might be able to buy some basic kits from a wholesaler which will be very popular given a little encouragement from your demonstrator.

Off-cuts

If you anticipate a good crowd including Dads and DIY enthusiasts (school fetes are good for this stall) have a timber sale. Gather all the off cuts that you can from friends and neighbours. Ask local builders or wood merchants to make donations. Put your stall near the car park so that people can get their purchases home easily or you could offer a delivery service.

Rings and things

Jewellery works well, but you will never be able to compete with the high street so keep your stall either very cheap and cheerful or unique craft work.

 **HANDY HINT**

Look for items that can be sold for pocket money prices – all under a pound – these are often available already attractively packaged in display trays from a wholesaler.

Paper goods

Cards and stationery goods are the one category where you should not restrict the price. For some reason, the bigger and more special the cards, the more popular they are, despite a high price tag. Local scenes, paintings on silk, pressed flowers or hand printed cards will all swell your funds. Look in the yellow pages for wholesalers or craft workers who will be delighted to sell you cards in large quantities. If you are very ambitious or know a good artist, you could commission three or four exclusive designs and get them printed. But you will be liable for a quite

PLUS & MINUS

- + Great way to use up jumble, extra produce and unwanted presents.
- + Easy to keep adding on to an existing event.
- + Often needs very little start-up costs.
- + Not difficult to organise.
- + Lots of attractive stalls can make an event in itself.
- + Rarely need more than two people to run each stall.

- – Might need to hire special equipment to run a side show, but usually it can be made at home.
- – Food stalls are subject to Food Safety regulations.
- – Bottle stalls and other games of chance are restricted by the terms of lotteries legislation.

considerable outlay before you see your money back. So make very sure of your market first.

Clothes

Knitwear and handmade clothes can both be money spinners, but aim for the youngster's market first. Adults are more fussy about a good fit. Children's clothes are cheaper and quicker to make too.

With all produce and goods stalls you will soon discover that some goods do better in some areas than others. It is only with experience that you will begin to get a feel for the popular items. In Norfolk, I know that in coastal areas people are looking for little presents, toys and sweets. Move inland into the countryside and children's clothes, plants and home-made produce go down well. In the cities and towns, you can be onto a winner with a jumble sale or a craft and handiwork fair. Your area might well be different so learn as you go, but don't be disappointed if your first event doesn't go quite the way you hoped.

Possible Problems?

Strictly speaking those stalls or games that are games of chance are governed by the rules of the Lotteries and Amusements Act 1976. As stated elsewhere in this book, and in detail in the chapter on Tax, Licences, Rules and Regulations, the new National Lottery Act 1993 is on the statute books and has just come into force so we must adjust to operate under the new legislation.

One of the most restrictive regulations is the cumulative prize rule which dictates that the value of all the prizes offered at one event – not just on one stall – must not exceed £250, see chapter on Raffles, Tombolas and Sweepstakes.

Under the same Act as mentioned above, you must not offer cash prizes. Of course the Matchbox House does just this. But is it a game of chance or skill? Perhaps you could get round this one by having the matchboxes unattached. Players could then pick them up and attempt to guess, by weighing them, how much the contain. If they are correct they keep the contents. Instead of cash fill them with sweets or pocket money presents.

EVENT 25 TROLLEY DASH

Winning raffle prize is free groceries

Operating requirements: Co-ordinator and treasurer. Volunteers to sell tickets.

Equipment needs: 500 tickets with stubs.

Lead time: Eight weeks.

Initial cost: £35 for registration under the Lotteries Act. Printing perforated draw tickets should cost about £40 and you will have advertising costs, allow another £50-£100, depending on how large you expect your draw to be. You may have to pay for the food which will come out of the proceeds.

Suitable for: Almost anything.

Expected return: A typical example might be, 500 tickets for £1.00 each = £500, less about £130 worth of goods and £40 for tickets gives you a balance of £330. This is just a small draw but if you set your sights high and you allow enough time to sell tickets your only restriction is the £10,000 limit set by law. Sometimes the store donates the food, but you can't bank on it.

What's in it for contributors: The chance of a big value prize that they have control over. i.e. it is their skill and speed that dictates the value of the prize.

Frequency: You are limited by the policy of your local Superstores and by the terms of the Lotteries Act, see below.

Special requirements: This is a game of chance open to the public and as such is covered by the Lotteries and Amusements Act 1976/National Lottery Act 1993. The event is likely to be classified as a 'society or social' lottery and registration is compulsory.

How does it work?

Tickets are sold as in a raffle. The prize is a one minute dash around a consenting Superstore piling as much into your trolley as you can. It really plays on people's greed, this one!

How do we get started?

First, you need to find a willing Supermarket manager. Usually the dash takes place just after closing time so that the store is empty of customers. Make sure that he is happy for you to advertise the dash and your charity around the store. Decide on a date for the draw and work backwards to establish your timescale.

You will need to apply for registration with your local authority at least four weeks before you put your tickets on sale. This will cost you £35 for the first year and £17.50 annual renewal (correct for 1993). If your group plan to hold several lotteries you will still only have to register once but you must hold no more than 52 in any year with a week between each one. Total proceeds must not exceed £20,000, before registering with the Gaming Board, and the largest prize until recently could not have a value in excess of £2,000; however the new National Lottery Act 1993 has now raised this to £25,000. Limits on the administration expenses are provided by statute and you need to check this against your budget. The promoter of the lottery must be a member of the society (charity) and every ticket should detail the name of the society and the name and address of the promoter. Tickets must also show the price of the ticket which must not exceed £1.00. Your local authority Licensing Department will be able to advise and help you with any problems.

Are there any exemptions?

Yes. Competitions are exempt from registration. Amazingly enough, even when there is a combination of luck and skill it is still classified as a competition.

So, hold your draw; but include a question of skill on the draw tickets. Something like 'Where was the first Safeway Store (if it is Safeway) opened?' or a multiple choice question such as 'How many tins of beans are sold in the UK every day? a, 10,000; b, 100,000 or c, 1 million'. The first correct entry drawn is the winner.

This is my and my friendly solicitor's interpretation of the law; but as with all legal matters, if in doubt, check it out. On the other hand £35 and a few weeks wait while the licence is sorted is no great hardship so you might prefer to run your dash in the conventional manner and get registered.

How do we sell tickets?

Have your tickets made up in books of twenty and give books to volunteers to sell tickets for you at least four weeks before the dash. There should also be a permanent place to buy tickets from within the store itself. Log the ticket numbers against each sales person and collect the money regularly to deposit in a separate bank or building society account. Make sure all stubs carry the name and address of the person who bought each individual number. This is most important as it would be impossible for everyone who bought a ticket to be present at the draw.

Start advertising a week or two before the tickets go on sale, to build up interest, using posters in and around the store. Give leaflets to the check-out staff to hand to each customer and send a press release to the local media and to the charity's local newsletter, if they have one. The store itself will often include the dash in its own advertising as it will encourage people to come to the store to buy a ticket and hopefully stock up on a few items as well.

How do we organise the draw?

Arrange for the draw to be made by a VIP, either someone from the store itself or the benefiting charity. If you set up some sort of platform with bunting or have a band playing outside the store for half an hour or so before the draw you may well make a fair quantity of last minute sales. Don't forget to inform the Police beforehand, they may have traffic reasons or know of conflicting events that might persuade you to be indoors or plan the draw for another day.

Use a 'roll-up man' with a megaphone to generate a feeling of urgency and a good audience. He can shout something like 'Only fifteen minutes left to buy your tickets for the fabulous, one minute, trolley dash to be held here, at (name of store) at precisely 5.00pm next Monday' or 'Just one pound, yes, one pound, for your chance to collect over a hundred pounds worth of groceries in one minute'.

Make an occasion of the draw and give the press (which you will have invited, of course) some good 'photo-opportunities' for the local paper so that they have an interesting trailer for the dash.

Borrow or hire a spinning barrel or tombola drum (addresses at the back of the book) in which you will have placed all the ticket stubs so that all the VIP has to do is spin the drum and draw the winning ticket.

PLUS & MINUS

- ⊞ Exciting event that doesn't take much organisation.
- ⊞ No venue hire.
- ⊞ Does not need many helpers other than volunteers to sell tickets.
- ⊞ Several media angles.
- ⊞ The supermarket will often donate the prize.
- ⊟ Might have trouble persuading managers to allow use of their store. Point out that they will take over £100 on the dash and there are many advertising opportunities.
- ⊟ Not suitable for young children, the elderly, or disabled people.
- ⊟ Have to be prepared to spend over £100 for the dash whether or not you sell the tickets.

How do we organise the actual dash?

You can set a date for the dash beforehand or you can wait until the draw to set the date. If your draw is a small one it would be kinder to leave setting a date until you are sure that your winner will be able to attend. If you need to fix a date you will need to work out whether you will accept a substitute 'dasher' if the winner cannot be present or if you will draw a second winner.

Send invitations to all you think might be interested. Local journalists, local radio, representatives of the benefiting charity or group will all want to know in advance who is the winner. Don't forget a senior manager from the Superstore's headquarters as well as the winner's family and friends.

Allow the winner to choose the trolley that s/he wants to use and let them decide where they want to start in the store. Wines, spirits and cigarettes are usually not included in the dash. Set the clock and ask someone special to start the run.

Arrange a photograph for the local rag of the exhausted winner with the pile of goods and run them through the check-out immediately to announce how much was won.

You might want to provide a glass of wine and some nibbles or perhaps the store might provide some refreshment if they are not contributing the goods.

The store may donate all the items in the trolley, they may donate the first £100 worth of goods out of their community budget or they may prefer to accept payment, but then donate the full amount to another charity of their choice. Make sure that they get some publicity out of their generosity also.

What happens afterwards?

Make sure that the store is sent a thank you letter along with anyone special that might have been involved.

EVENT 26

WISHING WELL

Exploitation of a desire to throw money into water

Operating requirements: Co-ordinator, treasurer. Three or four helpers.

Equipment needs: Water feature (see below for how to obtain).

Lead time: 1 month.

Initial cost: Very little although you may have to pay for electricity.

Suitable for: All charities. Needs to be situated in secure arcade, public building, large store or shopping mall.

Expected return: Entirely depends on quantity or generosity of passers-by.

What's in it for contributors: Satisfaction of a strange English desire to drop money into water. And, less cynically, something attractive and unusual to look at.

Frequency: Not worth doing for less than two weeks or so. A month would be ideal.

Special requirements: Power supply and secure venue.

How does it work?

This is not strictly a wishing well but I think the principle works just as effectively using a fountain or pool.

How many times have you walked past a fountain in a city square or a well at a heritage centre and seen people throwing money into it? I don't know why they do it, but they do. In droves. And that's without any invitation or sign. During 1992 the Friends of Norwich Castle Museum recovered £1,705 in small change from the well in the keep, so it is a popular occupation! How much more is to be made if you consciously encourage people to part with their spare cash?

This idea brings the well, or the fountain, to the people. They drop their money in, you clear it out regularly and distribute it to your charity causes. Simple isn't it?

How do we get started?

First decide on your venue. Try to find a convenient existing fountain or pool if you possibly can. Milton Keynes already has its own fountains and pools as do many other modern shopping centres, so perhaps you might obtain the use of something along these lines.

However, if you have a great venue but no 'wishing well' it is not impossible to provide your own. Beg or borrow a self contained water feature (the bigger the better) from a garden centre or garden furniture manufacturer. They get a month's worth of free advertising from this idea so they don't have to be totally altruistic and if you can offer a really spectacular venue you should have no problems borrowing something suitably eye catching.

You won't need a water supply as most water features are self sufficient, i.e. the water is pumped round and round and once you have filled it you need only the occasional top-up. However, you will need an electrical supply if you include a fountain, to power the pump. Make sure that your supply is brought in safely. If you are indoors you should be able to position your fountain so as to prevent people tripping over the cable. An arcade might present more of a problem and you may have to consider 'flying' the cable across the rafters and dropping it down beside the feature. Other Malls may have power points strategically placed at floor level perhaps to run temporary lights at Christmas.

Ideally your water area should be wide enough to see lots of coins but deep enough to discourage theft unless thieves are determined enough to actually climb in and get their trousers wet. By that time you are in a position of superiority and you can hold their heads under long enough to get your money back! I think that might be classified as assault... but you get the gist.

What if you don't have a convenient, secure shopping mall available? A large museum might be helpful or perhaps you could persuade the owners of a theme park to let you use their entrance. I've also seen this idea work very successfully in the main entrance to a large department store or maybe a busy train station might be the answer. Think big, and use an area that expects hundreds of visitors a day.

HANDY HINT

You could use the opportunity to mount a small exhibition for a few days to show how previous funds have been used. Specify a particular project and a target figure to be raised at this appeal. People are more prepared to give to something particular rather than to a general charitable cause.

Do we need to advertise?

You are relying on passing trade to contribute to your cause. People are not going to go more than a few yards out of their way to throw money away. You have about five seconds to make an impact, which is about what it takes for someone to walk past and glance in your direction. You need to have immediate appeal and get your message across in just a few words.

Have a couple of signs professionally sign-painted displaying something like the box, right.

You can use a couple of easels to show your signs off to good advantage and allow the sponsorship companies (the supplier of the water feature, the owners of the arcade, and the shop supplying the electricity, for instance) a leaflet stand to advertise goods and services.

You don't need to print posters or pay for advertisements. As with almost any fundraising idea, you do need to exploit any public relations potential and send properly prepared press releases out. Follow up all releases with a telephone call to invite photographs or suggest an interview and let the journalists know that you will come back to them at the end of the appeal with the amount raised.

HELP SICK CHILDREN

(name of charity)

WISHING WELL

Make a wish!

Sponsored by

JACK BEANSTALK

(name of garden centre)

PLUS & MINUS

- + No committee or lengthy organisation needed.
- + Very little outlay or advertising needed.
- + Can run for several weeks with little supervision.
- − Relies on finding just the right venue and perhaps persuading someone to lend you a valuable piece of equipment.
- − Relies on a regular commitment from someone to empty, count and bank money collected.
- − Not suitable for children's involvement, although children may number amongst your most generous contributors.

Do we need to provide supervision?

My feeling is not, or at least not all the time. If your venue is fairly well supervised by staff members in nearby shops or has security cameras you may be able to visit only occasionally, perhaps at lunch time when the area is most popular or later in the afternoon when your haul is at its most vulnerable. You will be the best judge of safety at your venue, but in any case you can change your plans as the days go on. There is bound to be the odd person who thinks they will just help themselves to some cash, but in my experience most potential thieves don't think it is worth getting wet for some loose change.

Make sure that the appropriate people know who will be collecting the money at the end of each day. You don't want to have to bail a bonafide charity helper out of prison.

Whilst you won't need a patrol, if you have borrowed your water feature you will have to make sure that it is secure each evening. All electricity should be switched off and you must be able to assure the owners that their precious fountain won't go walkabout. There are serious minded criminals about who are prepared to drive trucks into town centres at night for the sole purpose of removing concrete planters, cast iron litter bins and benches. It is important, for this reason, that you choose a venue that is locked up at night. Check that any insurance isn't invalidated by your presence and that you have any necessary cover for yourselves.

What happens at the end?

You must thank every one involved, of course. Write letters and let them know how much was raised. If you sense that they were pleased with their involvement, make a tentative suggestion that you might work together again in the future, but avoid the temptation to pin them down at this stage.

Ensure that all equipment goes back clean and in good condition and be there personally when they come to collect it.

PLUS ANOTHER TWENTY-SIX QUICK AND EASY IDEAS

Organising full scale fundraising events can be very hard work and time consuming and not for everyone. Maybe you have had a hand in several large scale events and you feel it is time you took a back seat, or perhaps your family has got to 'that stage' – all under five – and is draining you of the last dregs of energy and opportunity. Sometimes we still feel we would like to be involved and are committed to a particular cause but need to take a more low key approach. The following ideas are for you. You are never going to make thousands of pounds in a couple of weeks but you will be able to provide a small but valuable and steady flow of funds to your cause and perhaps gain a little public awareness each time someone cares to ask what it is all about. Don't feel guilty about not always volunteering for the major role on a committee or taking on the same event, just because it is expected. You can pick one or two of the ideas below and explain that you will still be contributing.

Appeals

Your contribution can be by using a letter, a press advertisement or a leaflet. Do as much or as little as you can manage but do work out a strategy first; you need every message to leave its mark.

Baby sitting

Perhaps you could let it be known that you are available to baby-sit every Friday or every second Tuesday of the month, or whatever. Charge a realistic fee and donate the proceeds.

Bulb growing

Good to run this idea through a club, society or school. Charge to enter, perhaps a garden centre would donate the bulbs, if not they are supplied by the competitors. The tallest plant by a certain day wins a prize. Swell funds by sponsoring the plants by the centimetre.

Coffee morning

Hold an 'open-house' for members of your community. Charge for coffee and biscuits or cake. Ask people to donate cakes or if you have a large party you might need to take expenditure from the proceeds.

Collection box

Keep a collection box in your house by the front door.

Double or nothing

Give a sum of money to members of a club to double (or more) within a certain time. £1 to buy a packet of seeds to grow £5 worth of vegetables. £2 to buy wool for a child's jumper to sell at £4 and so on.

Dressing-up for sale

Children love dressing-up in Mum's old clothes. Ask a group of Mums to a bring and buy party to fill the dressing-up boxes with loopy clothes and hats.

Empties

There are not so many bottles with 'money-back' on them any more but they can be found. Recycling cans can bring in money and there are companies that still collect stamps. You might be able to collect trading stamps that people leave behind at petrol stations or at Co-Operative stores.

Foreign stamps

Have a sale of duplicates in your house or at a club.

Friends club

People pay a subscription to belong to an official group associated with your organisation. They also pledge to fundraise in turn.

Gardening

Make it known that you are available to help in the garden for a couple of hours each week for two months. Charge a reasonable rate and donate all or part of the proceeds.

Go-karting

Take a minibus full of keen karters to one of the local centres that you will find in your Yellow Pages. Ask if you can get a group discount and explain that you are a charitable organisation. You might get some columns in the local rag for the Kart company especially if you take a 'personality'. Charge individuals the full price and use the profit. This idea can be used for all sorts of activities: sailing, riding, roller skating etc.

Hitchin' box

Put a collection box in the car for passengers to make their contributions. Make sure that you don't leave it in view when you park your car.

Home made goods

Organise a bring and buy sale in your front room or garden of cakes, jams, sweets, vegetables etc.

Lawn mowing race

Great idea if you need a community area's grass cut. You save money in not paying a contractor and you can either sponsor mowers or charge an entry to compete.

Lecture service

If you are an expert in your field or have something interesting to talk about, offer your services for charity as a speaker.

Newspaper collection

Not confined to newspapers. Offer to collect people's recyclables for a small fee. Make it known that you will be calling in a particular area on a certain day.

Office appeal

It is surprising how much can be raised in just one day if you walk a collecting box around a large office or factory. Don't forget the canteens.

Organise an outing

Take a group on a nature walk or a picnic, they pay to take part of course.

Photo flash

If you are a dab hand with a camera, offer to take pictures at a the school fete or local street procession. Take orders for pictures at a coffee morning and profits after your expenses go to your charity.

Plant sale

Offer plants or cuttings for sale in your garden to any visitors or hold a bring and buy plant party.

Roadside sale

If you have a productive garden you might be prepared to run a stall for excess produce. Leave the goods bundled or bagged into small amounts and provide an honesty box. You might need a street trading permission if your stall is on the pavement, though not if it is within your garden.

Universal helping hands

A group of people who are willing to help anybody out in the locality for money. You need to have a central number to ring and someone to co-ordinate the helpers.

Visit a month

A regular collection from the homes of people who have pledged to give so much over a specified period of time.

Window cleaning

People usually have a regular external window cleaner but often don't get around to doing the insides. A dependable and trusted local person to see to the interiors would be a great help to many folks.

Xmas draw

Organise a special Christmas raffle to be drawn at a local shop on Christmas Eve. You will need to register with the local authority (see chapter on Raffles).

APPENDIX:

TAX, LICENCES, RULES AND REGULATIONS

TAX

V.A.T.

One-off or annual fundraising efforts are usually exempt from VAT. However, if you choose to run your enterprise as a shop, even if you open as little as once a month or run your events as part of a series, you will have to register for VAT as soon as your annual turnover reaches the £45,000 threshold. If you are doing this well you probably won't mind having to register! But be aware that you are not automatically exempt because you are a charity, although there are exceptions. If you are spectacularly successful at running Coffee mornings or Jumble sales in the same hall each week, for instance, and you reach the registration threshold you will not be accountable for VAT as it is thought that the risk of competition to local business is marginal.

A final word if you are fundraising for a school. Make sure that your purchase orders are on official, numbered LEA order forms (unless your school has opted for local management). You will be charged VAT on all invoices and county councils can claim this back, but only against official orders.

Gift Aid

Gift Aid was introduced by John Major when he was Chancellor. Very briefly, if a taxpaying individual makes a donation of £250 or more to a charity, that payment will be regarded as having been made net of basic rate tax. This means that the charity will be able to claim a repayment of tax and the donor will be able to claim higher rate relief, if appropriate. The gift must be a 'qualifying donation' within the meaning of Section 25 of the Finance Act 1990. The Inland Revenue have brought out a guidance booklet, see back of the book for details.

CHARITIES ACT 1993

There are some fairly fundamental points of law that are raised by the introduction of the new Charities Act 1993 which updated and consolidated aspects of earlier legislation and the Charities Act 1992; they are too detailed and too numerous to go into in detail in this publication.

However, there are certain requirements that any fundraiser should be aware of and seek further advice if necessary.

What is a charity?

A charity can exist without necessarily applying for registration: indeed you may be operating with 'charitable purposes' as defined in law without even knowing it. Even in ignorance you are still required to observe charity law and are able to receive the tax benefits that are due to registered charities. Clearly, then it is within your interests to obtain official recognition and have a flexible constitution drawn up professionally which allows you the freedom to fundraise how you wish.

Registration

Registering as a charity is now compulsory for any charity which has a permanent endowment, or uses and occupies land, or whose income from all sources is £1,000 or more. There are certain exemptions and exceptions relating to churches, certain museums, universities and schools. If you are fundraising for an exempt body it might be more sensible to fundraise under their umbrella rather than have to register because you have set yourselves up as a separate organisation.

Registration is fairly straight forward and the Charity Commission for your area will advise you on procedure.

It is preferable to set your fundraising up as a charitable body, or under an umbrella organisation, rather than running each event in watertight compartments as completely separate fundraising operations; the reason being as follows. If you run two events, and event A makes a profit and event B makes a loss, you cannot recover your losses on the second event, or even the third (to be held in the future), unless the money is being raised for the organisation that is running the event, and that organisation subsequently donates the money to the eventual beneficiary. Again, you see my interest in flexibility.

Requirements pertinent to fundraising

All registered charities must state the fact that they are registered on all stationary (but not, rather surprisingly, cheques). If you gross more than £5,000 a year you must state the registration number on all literature, including cheques. You should also state what it is that you are fundraising for. And this is where your legal advice is important. Should you need £2,000 for a particular project and you raise over your goal, what do you do with the surplus? You need the wording to be flexible enough to allow you to roll it over into another project, put it on deposit, pay for a survey or whatever you need.

Whether you are registered or not you must have proper accounts. Any member of the public has a right to see the books within two months of a written request. You can charge a small fee for postage and photocopying.

All your activities must be for charitable purposes within the four categories as stated in the Act, and those activities must be within your stated objects.

The charity can only trade for its own charitable purposes; political activities are restricted and must be directly relevant.

Professional fundraisers

Finally, a point about employing professional fundraisers. Whilst the majority of professional fundraisers do a very good and invaluable job there have been unscrupulous individuals who have entered the business for the express purposes of lining their own pockets. The problem was addressed in the Charities Act 1992 Part II which comes into force in 1994. The Act states that it will be an offence for any professional fundraiser to solicit funds for charity unless they have signed a formal agreement as prescribed by the regulations. If you are considering employing a professional fundraiser you should take advice about payment – percentages, commission or set fees, control of funds and insolvency. Whatever you do, don't employ anyone without following up two or three references.

LICENCES

Public Entertainment Licences

The law (Local Government, Miscellaneous Provisions, Act 1982) states that where two or more people are performing and/or dancing is involved, a Public Entertainments Licence is required. The main areas of concern are the safety of the electrical system, any potential fire hazards and the availability of fire escapes, exits and procedures for emptying the building, and noise pollution. Inside and outside events may be treated rather differently but the concerns will not change.

Shows that include a hypnotism act or live animals may be banned or restricted in certain Local Authority areas; it is worth getting advice if you are hiring a council-owned venue as inclusion could affect the granting of a licence.

Inside events: These tend to be potentially more hazardous when held in a previously unlicensed building. If, however, you have chosen a public building in which to hold your event such as a Church Hall, pub or Community centre then you may well find that the building already holds a Public Entertainments Licence and all you have to do is comply with the terms previously agreed. For something like a Ceilidh held in the local farmer's barn or a concert in the village church a temporary Public Entertainments Licence will have to be sought. You will need to apply at least three months in advance to allow time for re-submission if you are at first unsuccessful.

Do not even think of applying if you can not guarantee several fire exits or if your venue backs on to a noise sensitive building such as a hospital or sheltered accommodation.

Outside events: Generally speaking if musical entertainment is not the main attraction, the authorities are not really interested. If you are expecting a crowd of more than a few hundred people it might be

PROCEDURES IN APPLYING FOR A PUBLIC ENTERTAINMENTS LICENCE

a. Visit the Local Authority relevant to the area in which you plan to hold the event. Ask to see someone from the Licensing Section of the Administration Department or make an appointment.

b. You will be given several copies (at least 5 or 6) of a form on which you should specify the type of licence that you require – usually music and dancing. The Enforcement Officer should be happy to advise you. You will also be asked to give the name and address of the venue and your (the applicant's) name and address and a plan of the building or site that you intend to use. There may also be a space to add the date of the licensing committee that you wish to consider the application. There will be a charge of between £100 and £250 depending on the Authority.

c. The copies are sent variously to the Chief Fire Officer, the Police, the Environmental Health Department and the remainder to the Licensing Officer.

d. You will also be asked to submit an electrical certificate, perhaps separately to the Environmental Health Department. This is usually arranged and paid for by the promoter and can be quite expensive according to the size of the building or rig used. At the time of writing (1993) £175+ is the going rate. The inspection must be carried out by a qualified electrician and one who is approved by the licensing authority so make sure that you do your homework first.

e. Then comes the wait. Before the committee hears your application you may well have a visit from one or more of the interested bodies to hear about your event in more detail. If your event is outside you will be unable to supply certain information or an electrical certificate as the infrastructure will not be in place – so expect a decision to be made with conditions.

f. You may well be ordered to advertise the date and nature of the event in the local press and by poster outside your proposed venue (at your own expense). This is to enable potential complainants to come forward to have their comments taken into consideration when the committee meets.

g. If your application is successful you can proceed according to plan. If the application is successful but conditions are imposed you will have to show that these can be met – often on the day of the event – and an officer will make arrangements to inspect just hours before you open to the public. S/he has the right to prevent the show from opening or restrict part of it, although in practice, it is unlikely that this will happen if your venue is not actively dangerous.

prudent to take advice should you be planning a DJ and disco as part of the fun; it is just possible that in urban areas complaints will have been made before and the Environmental Protection Officers may be more sensitive than usual.

If you plan an event to comprise largely of performers you will certainly have to apply for a Public Entertainments Licence and, as for inside events, plan to apply for this at least three months in advance.

Liquor or Justices' Licences

If you wish to sell alcohol, or intoxicating liquor as it is legally called, at your event you will have to be licensed. The decision to grant a licence is made by the local Magistrates Court who take advice from the Police. If you are holding a show in a building that already has a licensed bar

PROCEDURES FOR APPLYING FOR A LIQUOR OR JUSTICE'S LICENCE

Having found your tame landlord, the procedure is as follows:

a. Applications are made to the Magistrates Court, giving details of the event itself, the venue and what area is to covered by the licence. (This could be just the immediate bar area or include a fenced off seating area outside a tent). S/he will be required to give one month's notice, although in practice, if you are desperate for a licence your Court may well be able to give you a decision within 48 hours.

b. You will be given 3 copies of the application form one of which has to sent to the Police, so that they have a chance to object. The other two are returned to the Court.

c. Most Courts have a sitting twice a week to decide on licences and you should be informed fairly promptly by letter as to which way the hearing went. If your event is less than one month from the sitting you will be asked to attend the hearing so you will know the decision instantly. Incidentally, if you fail to show up at the court when you have specifically been asked to attend your application may automatically be turned down.

d. In some cases the Police will not recommend refusal of the licence but they might put restrictions on it. For instance the Lord Mayor's Street Procession in Norwich has traditionally been granted a licence for a beer tent in the city centre gardens but in recent years this has been the site of rowdiness and underage drinking and the Police have imposed conditions to try and limit these problems. The licensee has had to agree to all alcohol being sold in open disposable 'glasses' (so that tins cannot be passed to underage consumers) and the beer tent had to have an area fenced off to prevent drink being consumed all over the park; a full hour has also been knocked off the opening times. This was not a popular decision but has, nevertheless, helped to solve the problems. It was a case of comply or no licence.

then provided that the licensee is in charge of the bar during the event you will have no problems.

Outside, or in an unlicensed building you can apply for an occasional liquor licence which will cost you about £4.00 and you can hold up to four events in the same year on that licence. You will be asked many searching questions and might be restricted to beer or wine only. If there is any doubt as to your suitability or the suitability of the event the licence will be denied. I feel that the best way of obtaining permission to open your bar should be to approach a licensee who already holds a full 'on-licence' and ask him/her to apply for you. This is quite legal and indeed the Police welcome this action as the landlord is, in effect, asking to extend the area of his/her pub for the duration of the event. You will also have access to wholesale priced liquor.

Street Collection Permits

The terms of a Street Collection Permit have been covered in the chapter on Street Collections and Flag Days.

You will be required to apply, in writing, to the Administration Department of the Council covering the area in which the collection is to be held at least one month prior to the event, and possibly a great deal earlier than that if you want to be sure of booking the day you need.

REQUIREMENTS FOR BEING GRANTED A COLLECTION PERMIT

Generally, the basis on which a permit is granted is as follows:

a. Only one organisation to collect each day and that group must only collect on the allotted day and between the times as stated on the permit and in the permitted place. (The permitted place may be the whole of the town centre or it could be restricted to just one street).

b. People carrying collecting boxes should remain stationary and must not coerce passers-by or show intimidating behaviour.

c. Collections have to be made in sealed boxes – usually available from the benefiting charity – although many authorities are tolerant when it comes to using buckets etc. in moving processions or at Fun Runs, for instance.

d. All collectors must be aged 16 (18 in London) or over and be acting voluntarily. They must wear badges and carry authorisation from the promoter.

After the collection you will be asked to complete a form giving the Council information including the total amount collected, who counted it, and a list of all the collectors etc.

Legislation as described above will be replaced shortly by Part III of the Charities Act 1992 (Sections 65-74) with the new legislation regulating what will be known as 'Public Charitable Collections'. Regulations should be published late 1994, and will cover definitions of a 'public place' (see Street Collections chapter). Specifically excluded from the definition of a 'public place' is any place to which a ticket must be purchased to gain access or where permission is given for the purposes of the appeal.

The regulations, when published, are likely to cover matters relating to the keeping and publication of accounts, prevention of annoyance, wearing of badges and carrying of certificates by collectors who must be over certain ages.

Lottery registration

A lottery is any game of chance in which tickets are sold enabling the holder to possibly qualify for a prize or money. This could include raffles, sweepstakes, tombolas, etc. Games of chance are covered by the Lotteries and Amusements Act 1976 and the National Lottery Act 1993. When you introduce an element of skill such as in 'Spot the Ball' or 'Guess the weight of the cake' it then becomes a competition and is not subject to such rigorous regulations. In simple terms there are three types of lotteries that an event organiser might be interested in.

Private Lotteries: whilst of a more limited fundraising potential, these are far less regulated than any other type of lottery. It must be confined to members of a club or society with the net proceeds of the lottery being used to provide prizes to further the work of the society. The lottery can only be advertised on the society's premises but there is no limit to the size of the lottery or on the price of the tickets. The price of every ticket shall, however, be stated on the ticket and every ticket shall bear the name and address of the promoter and a statement detailing the people to whom the sale of tickets is restricted. Each ticket shall also state that no prize won shall be paid or delivered to any person other than the person who bought the winning ticket. Tickets can only be allocated by way of sale and this must be done in person and cannot be conducted through the post.

Small Lotteries: these must not be the main attraction of an event. They must be incidental to an 'exempt entertainment' such as a bazaar, dinner dance, sporting event etc. The lottery must then take place on the premises where the main entertainment takes place and there must be no element of private gain in the running of either the lottery or the entertainment. Prizes must not exceed £250 in value; this is at the whole event – not just one bottle stall, for example – and shall not be paid in cash. Subject to the above there is no limit on the size of the lottery or on the price of the tickets, although tickets can only be sold during the progression of the event and in the case of a raffle or tombola the draw must take place before the end and on the same premises.

Social or Society Lotteries: for a more effective lottery involving the sale of tickets over a period of time you will need to go through the process of registration with the Local Authority (usually through the Licensing or Administration Department). This is really only cost effective if your group is to hold regular lotteries. It currently (1993) costs £35 for initial registration, which covers you until the next 1st January when a renewal fee of £17.50 is payable. Unless you apply for cancellation a renewal fee is due every New Year. The registration allows you to hold a lottery as follows:

a. Registration is only possible if you are already an established group and fundraising for charitable purposes.

b. If the Authority agrees to registration a certificate will be granted, but you have the right to appeal if your group is not successful.

c. Proceeds must not exceed £20,000 and prizes may only be offered up to £25,000 in amount or value. If you exceed these limits your lottery must also be registered with the Gaming Board who charge a fee of £510.

d. Expenses may be appropriated providing they are accurate and not more than 30%* of the proceeds.

e. You may hold up to 52 lotteries in a year.

f. You must only sell tickets to people of 16 or over.

g. Each ticket or chance should be sold at a price of £1.00 or under; every ticket should be the same and show the cost on the ticket itself.

h. Each prize should be offered against one ticket only.

i. The promoter must be a member of the society (charity) and every ticket shall specify the name of the society and the name and address of the promoter.

j. Afterwards, the promoter must make a return to the Local Authority on the form provided.

* The National Lottery Act 1993 is now in force but some associated regulations are not yet issued. In particular there will be changes to the registration requirements, ticket prices and values, prize amounts and expenses allowed.

Generally, there is expected to be a relaxation in the rules which should enable charities and societies to make better use of fundraising opportunities provided by lotteries.

There are, of course, other more specific rules but these are the regulations germane to the operation of any lottery. If you are seriously considering registration there is a helpful leaflet on the Lotteries and Amusements Act – Cat No. B.L.5 from Shaw & Sons Ltd. (address at the back of the book) which may also be available from any Local Authority.

If you are concerned or worried about any exemption or procedure involving raffles or lotteries a quick call to your District Council should clarify things.

OTHER RULES AND REGULATIONS

Competitions

Lotteries seem to be the more popular form of additional entertainment at many events. But when you consider the regulations and restrictions that surround them it is surprising that competitions are not more popular.

Competitions include any activity where the outcome of the event is decided by the skill or judgement of the player. Even where there is a mixture of skill and luck this is still classified as a competition. A draw to win a boat is a typical example. The draw alone would not be legal if the prize is worth more than the £25,000 limit. But introduce a tie-break sentence for the two potential winners pulled out of the hat, and you now have a perfectly legal competition.

There are no restrictions on the amount of money taken or any limit on the value of the prizes. Indeed you at liberty to offer cash prizes. So my advice is to forget lotteries; go for competitions every time.

One word of warning, for all the above, Section 14 of the original 1976 Act covers competitions and in particular competitions run in Newspapers and for commercial profit. However, in my opinion competitions held at charitable events will be exempt from this section. But, again, if you are in doubt check with your local authority.

Public areas, footpaths and rivers

Public areas and footpaths are often covered by local bye-laws and if there are conditions covering these they will be pointed out in the contract if you are hiring a council-owned venue.

The sort of bye-laws that may affect you are whether you are allowed to fence off a footpath or indeed an entire public area (usually provision is made in the bye-law for a prescribed number of days closure per year) or you may be advised that no event can be held between certain hours or even that you have to leave the children's playground free for public use.

Concessionary cafes or shops can also cause problems, sometimes restricting the use of further caterers or food vans. Most Recreation Departments will cover these points for you but you do need to be aware of what might be the complaint when the Park Cafe manager starts shouting at you and waving his arms about in fury.

If you plan to use the stream or river at the bottom of your site for entertainment e.g. a raft race or boat procession, it may be that you will need permission from the local River or Waterways Authority. If the water is navigable you will certainly have to speak to them before you plan anything. Your local council can advise you where to go for help as they will be in constant communication with the correct organisation and will know the potential problems.

Health and Safety at Work

The Health and Safety at Work Act is not only concerned with people in a formal place of work engaged in paid work for a registered company or individual. It is a 'catch all' law that is intended to protect everybody and anybody who is working with the public, paid or voluntarily. It is also particularly concerned with protecting third parties, for example the innocent passer-by who has something fall on his head from above. If an accident occurs as a result of activities taking place because of your event the investigating authority will be looking for someone on whom to pin the blame and prosecute. That will almost certainly be the organising group of the event.

Any activity that involves scaffolding or building work of any kind will be classified as 'construction' and the laws surrounding this work are very stringent. If you are using scaffolding or towers, even to make a small grandstand for instance, you would be well advised to have it erected professionally, thus taking the onus off yourselves.

Any group organising any event other than a few stalls or teas and games should study a very readable and clear government publication called 'Essentials of Health and Safety at Work'. All types of work and activity are covered and it gives very practical and easy-to-use guidelines on avoiding hazards and what to do in emergencies. It is a sobering thought that every year over 500 people lose their lives whilst engaged in work activities and thousands more are injured or suffer work-induced illness.

Fairgrounds and Safety Certificates

Most fairgrounds are owned by professional showmen. You can sometimes book individual rides but more usually you employ the whole works – rides, stalls, candyfloss pitches, everything. You can let them come onto the site free of charge as an added attraction but most showmen will think it worth their while to pay £200 – £300 for the pitch. Showmen can be intimidating if you have never worked with them before and you need to be clear what it is that you require from them and what they expect from you and what your rights are.

Most showmen prefer to work the sites that they are familiar with and in the main they are likely to turn up as planned if they are not going to somewhere new, especially if they have paid a pitch fee in advance, but you cannot always rely on them. This may seem unfair to those fairground operators who always behave honourably, but this is my opinion after many years working with showmen.

If the event is organised by you or your club and a fair is present at your invitation it is your responsibility to check the safety of the site. It will be your insurance which has to pay up if there is an accident. Every ride has an annual inspection, rather like an MOT, and is given a certificate if it is safe. You have a right to see all the certificates. You will also have to ensure that the site is safe after the fair is set up. You will need to arrange for an inspector who is a member of the National Association for Leisure Industry Certificates to visit the site a few hours before it opens to the public. You can ask for a list of qualified inspectors from your local Health and Safety Office or your local council may well employ a qualified engineer themselves; most of the time this is not a problem but in East Anglia, uniquely, they are few and far between so you will need to book somebody well in advance if your event is in this area. This is arranged at the showmen's expense and they know that they will have to pay the electrician before they can be issued with a Safety Certificate.

You can give the area the once-over before the inspector comes so that you can point out anything that worries you. The sort of things that you should be looking for are whether the gangways are clear and wide enough to get the emergency services through if needed. Are all the cables heavy duty and weather proof? If they cross gangways they need to be flown above seven feet or dug into the ground so that they cannot be tripped over. Do the rides look well maintained or are safety rails missing or moving parts unprotected?

If you are unhappy with any aspect of your fair or the behaviour of the showmen running it you can complain to the Showman's Guild of Great Britain – your local section secretary will be listed in the telephone directory.

Inflatable castles

At present there are no laws governing bouncy castles but I feel it will not be long before this is looked at. There have been some truly appalling accidents in recent years – over 4,000 children are injured annually in the UK – through negligence and thoughtless use; absolutely anybody can buy a castle and set themselves up as a hire company with no training or registration. Inflatable castles or rides should be tied down with guyropes, as in even the lightest of breezes they can take off and scatter children onto the ground resulting in injury or at the very least cause them to be very frightened, and use should be cancelled completely in rain due to the slippery surfaces. One adult should always be present within the castle to help children if they panic or are jumped on. Times restricted to certain age groups and limiting children on the castle at any one time to a safe number can all help keep accidents to a minimum, but the children still need supervision. If there seems to be any problem at all with the blower or the possibility of a puncture, the castle should be cleared until it is certain that the castle is fully inflated and likely to stay that way.

You may also be aware of the new 'Bar Jump' or 'Sticky Castles' that are now available. These have been very popular in Australia and look like a regular castle except that the flat back to the rear of the inside is covered in very strong velcro. The 'bouncers' wear velcro suits and after working up their bouncing to a good height they then throw themselves at the sticky wall and stick: like flies in a spiders web! It is great fun and reasonably safe as long as no more than two jumpers are taking part at a time. Restrict times to about 5 minutes each. In my experience people, especially adults, will have had enough long before the time is up. It is one of the most exhausting activities that I have ever tried.

Whilst there are no statutory regulations as yet the Health and Safety Executive have recently issued detailed safety guidelines. HSE Guidance Note PM76 is available from HMSO stockists.

Insurance

You are not required by law to take out Public liability Insurance, but you would be very ill-advised to run any event to which the public have access without some sort of insurance. Premiums are really very small. About £25 should see you covered for an indemnity limit of £500,000 for a one day event. You can also insure against rain or loss of earnings.

There are many specialised insurance companies that deal with individual or unique needs. For a general insurance cover, Cornhill Insurance is as good as you will find, but go through a broker to ensure all your needs are provided for.

KEY POINTS

- Decide if you need to register for VAT.
- Remember the advantages of Gift Aid when asking for donations.
- Ensure that public safety is not jeopardised and that you are not infringing people's basic rights.
- If you are selling alcohol you will need a Justices' Licence.
- If you are holding an event where singing or dancing is the main attraction you will require a Public Entertainment Licence.
- Check that your raffle or lottery is exempt from the terms of the National Lottery Act or register with the local authority.
- Consider competitions in favour of lotteries.
- Check before you apply for any licence that your event is not likely to run into problems. You will have to pay the application fee whether or not the licence is granted.
- Enquire about your council's attitude to Sunday trading.
- Remember that the Health and Safety at Work Act covers ALL activities that take place in the public domain.
- Make yourself aware of any local bye-laws that may affect you.
- Don't forget to register well in advance if you plan to have a collection in a public place.
- If you are using a commercial fair make sure that every ride has it's 'MOT' and that you obtain a Safety Certificate for the whole fairground.
- Be aware of the dangers of inflatable castles.
- Ensure that you have adequate insurance cover.

NOTE:

All the information that is included in this chapter is given in good faith. It has been checked by a lawyer but I, and he, would like to point out that some areas are covered by regulations rather than Acts of Parliament and are subject to change at short notice. Take separate legal advice wherever possible and use this chapter to alert you to possible problems.

USEFUL PUBLICATIONS

Tax

GIFT AID – A Guide for Donors and Charities Inland Revenue booklet IR113, available from your local Tax Office.

TAX EFFECTIVE GIVING
by Michael Norton, published by The Directory of Social Change, available from The Directory of Social Change, Radius Works, Back Lane, London, NW3 1HL Tel:(071) 284 4364. Price £9.95

A PRACTICAL GUIDE TO VAT FOR CHARITIES
by Kate Sayer, published by The Directory of Social Change, available from The Directory of Social Change, Radius Works, Back Lane, London, NW3 1HL Tel:(071) 284 4364. Price £9.95

VAT LEAFLET 701/1/92 available from H.M. Customs and Excise Office

INLAND REVENUE LEAFLETS (free from your local tax office): IR113 A Guide for Donars and Charities; IR64 Giving to Charity – How Businesses can get Tax Relief; IR65 Giving to Charity – How Individuals can get tax Relief; IR75 Tax Relief for Charities.

The Charities Act

CHARITIES: LAW AND PRACTICE
by Eizabeth Cairns, published by Sweet and Maxwell, South Quay Plaza, 183 Marsh Wall, London EC14 9FT. Price £46.00

CHARITY LEAFLETS (available from the Charity Commission): CC20 Fundraising and Charities; CC21 Starting a Charity; CC25 Charities Acts 1960 and 1985 – Charity Accounts; CC27 Provision of Alcohol on Charity Premises; CC45 Central Register of Charities – Services Available.

Other regulations

'AND JUDY WILL RUN THE CAKE STALL' available free of charge with a SAE from Parkinson Cowen Brochure Services, 636 Bristol Road South, Birmingham, B31 2JR

THE FOOD SAFETY ACT, 1990 AND YOU – A GUIDE FOR THE FOOD INDUSTRY published by H.M.Government, available from Food Sense, London SE99 7TT Tel:(081) 694 8862

GUIDELINES FOR THE CATERING INDUSTRY ON THE FOOD HYGIENE (AMENDMENT) REGULATIONS 1990 AND 1991 published by the Department of Health, available from HMSO Bookshops

THE FOOD HYGIENE (MARKETS, STALLS AND DELIVERY VEHICLES) REGULATIONS 1996 AS AMMENDED BY THE FOOD HYGIENE (AMENDMENT) REGULATIONS 1990 published by Eaton Publications, P.O. Box 34, Walton-on-Thames, Surrey, Tel:(0932) 229001

ESSENTIALS OF HEALTH AND SAFETY AT WORK published by the Health and Safety Executive, available from HMSO Bookshops

LOTTERIES AND AMUSEMENTS ACT, 1976 – Cat No. BL5 published by Shaw and Sons Ltd, Shaway House, Lower Syndham, SE26 5AE

LOTTERIES & THE LAW, published by the Gaming Board for Great Britain, Berkshire House, 168–173 High Holborn, London WC1V 7AH

GUIDE TO HEALTH, SAFETY AND WELFARE AT POP CONCERTS AND OTHER SIMILAR EVENTS available from the Health and Safety Executive, Baynards House, 1 Chepstow Place, London W2 4TF

RECREATION AND THE LAW by Valerie Collins, published by E & F N Spon, 11 New Fetter Lane, London EC4P 4EE. Price £13.95

HSE GUIDANCE NOTE PM76 – inflatable castles, available from HMSO. Tel:(021) 200 2461

Fundraising for Schools

SCHOOL FUNDRAISING – what you need to know, by Anne Mountfield, published by The Directory of Social Change, available from The Directory of Social Change, Radius Works, Back Lane, London, NW3 1HL Tel:(071) 284 4364. Price £9.95

Events and Ideas

ORGANISING LOCAL EVENTS by Sarah Passingham, published by The Directory of Social Change, available from The Directory of Social Change, Radius Works, Back Lane, London, NW3 1HL Tel:(071) 284 4364. Price £7.95

ENGINEERS OF THE IMAGINATION – THE WELFARE STATE HANDBOOK Edited by Tony Coult and Baz Kershaw, published by Methuen London Ltd, 11 New Fetter Lane, London EC4 4EE. Price £8.99

FUNDRAISING CAN BE FUN RAISING Great Ormond Street Children's Hospital Fundraising package. Available free of charge from Great Ormond Street Hospital.

THE COMPLETE FUNDRAISING HANDBOOK by Sam Clarke, published by the Directory of Social Change, Radius Works, Back Lane, London, NW3 1HL Tel:(071) 284 4364. Price £12.95

HOW TO RAISE FUNDS AND SPONSORSHIP by Chris McCallum, published by How To Books, Plymbridge House, Estover Road, Plymouth PL6 7PZ. Price £7.99

BARBEQUES by Carole Handslip, published by Merehurst Press, Ferry House, 51/57 Laccy Road, Putney, London SW15 1PR. Price £2.45

Committees and organising groups

GETTING ORGANISED by Christine Holloway and Shirely Otto, published by the National Council of Voluntary Organisations, available from the Directory of Social Change, Radius Works, Back Lane, London, NW3 1HL Tel:(071) 435 8171. Price £5.95

STARTING AND RUNNING A VOLUNTARY GROUP by Sally Capper, Judith Unell and Anne Weyman published by the National Council of Voluntary Organisations.

JUST ABOUT MANAGING by Sandy Merritt Adirondack published by the London Voluntary Service Council, available from the Directory of Social Change, Radius Works, Back Lane, London, NW3 1HL Tel:(071) 284 4364. Price £10.95

THE MANAGEMENT OF VOLUNTARY ORGANISATIONS published by Croner Publications Ltd. Croner House, London Road, Kingston-upon-Thames, Surrey, KT2 6SR. Tel:(081) 547 3333. This is a very large, looseleaf for easy update, publication and due to its rather high cost probably best looked for in a library. It is well worth studying on all sorts of topics.

THE DIRECTORY OF VOLUNTEERING AND EMPLOYMENT OPPORTUNITIES Directory of Social Change, Radius Works, Back Lane, London, NW3 1HL Tel:(071) 284 4364. Price £7.95. A publication on volunteers.

Professional entertainers and help

SHOWCALL DIRECTORY compiled and published by the Stage and Television Today, 47 Bermondsey Street, London, SE1 3XT Tel:(071) 403 1818. Price £18.00

THE SHOWMAN'S DIRECTORY compiled and published by Lance Publications, Brook House, Mint Street, Godalming, Surrey GU7 1HE Tel.(0483) 422184. Price £17.00

Publicity and Marketing

MARKETING: A HANDBOOK FOR CHARITIES by Dorothy and Alistair McIntosh, published by the Directory of Social Change, Radius Works, Back Lane, London, NW3 1HL Tel:(071) 284 4364. Price £7.95

A BASIC PR GUIDE by Dorothy and Alistair McIntosh, published by the Directory of Social Change, Radius Works, Back Lane, London, NW3 1HL Tel:(071) 284 4364. Price £7.95

Volunteers

ESSENTIAL VOLUNTEER MANAGEMENT by Rick Lynd and Steve McCurtey published July 94 by the Directory of Social Change, Radius Works, Back Lane, London, NW3 1HL Tel:(071) 284 4364. Price £14.95

THE VOLUNTEER CENTRE UK The centre is the national agency promoting volunteering and publishes a range of practical and technical information on recruiting and using volunteers. The Centre will be moving to London in 1994.

Sponsorship

ASSOCIATION FOR BUSINESS SPONSORSHIP OF THE ARTS / W H SMITH SPONSORSHIP MANUAL, available through W.H.S. Smith stores. Price £14.95

THE ARTS SPONSORSHIP HANDBOOK by David Fishel, published by the Directory of Social Change, Radius Works, Back Lane, London, NW3 1HL Tel:(071) 284 4364. Price £7.95

A GUIDE TO COMPANY GIVING 1993 edition, the facts and figures on over 1,300 large companies, edited by Michael and Nicola Eastwood, published by the Directory of Social Change, Radius Works, Back Lane, London, NW3 1HL Tel:(071) 284 4364. Price £14.95

THE MAJOR COMPANIES GUIDE, the giving and sponsorship programmes of the top 350 companies, edited by David Casson, published by the Directory of Social Change, Radius Works, Back Lane, London, NW3 1HL Tel:(071) 284 4364. Price £14.95

THE LONDON GRANTS GUIDE, edited by Nicola Parker and John Stephen, published by the Directory of Social Change, Radius Works, Back Lane, London, NW3 1HL Tel:(071) 284 4364. Price £12.50

WEST MIDLANDS GRANTS GUIDE, edited by Nicola Eastwood and Daren Felgate, published by the Directory of Social Change, Radius Works, Back Lane, London, NW3 1HL Tel:(071) 435 8171. Price £9.95

Special Needs – both participatory or as audience

THE CREATIVE TREE edited by Gina Levete, published by Michael Russell (Publishing) Ltd, The Chantry, Wilton, Salisbury, Wiltshire. Price £7.95

ARTS FOR EVERYONE by Anne Pearson, published by the Carnegie Trust, available from Centre on Environment for the Handicapped, 126 Albert Street, London NW1 7NF. Price £ 6.00

USEFUL ADDRESSES

Fundraising aids

Countryside Art
The Old Rectory, Swaby, Alford,
Lincs LN13 0BQ.
Tel: Swaby (0507) 480685
Special design and printing service specifically for schools but suppliers to all charities. Tea towels, peg bags, stationery etc.

Alucan Recycling
I-mex House, 52 Blucher Street,
Birmingham B1 1QU
Tel: (021) 633 4656
Aluminium can recycling

Peeks of Bournmouth Ltd
Riverside Lane, Tuckton, Christchurch,
Bournemouth, Dorset BH6 3LD
Tel: (0202) 4177777
Complete fundraising packages including games, novelties, Balloons, etc.

Wall's Carnival Stores Ltd
155/161 Caversham Road, Reading,
Berkshire RG1 8BB
Tel: (0734) 586727
Fundraising packages, as above – also balloon gas

OPAX International
81 Kirkstall Road, Leeds LS3 1LH
Tel: (0532) 443636
Scratch cards

Carousel Fun Fairs Agency
Plot 24, The Plantation, West Park Road,
Newchapel, Surrey RH7 6HT
Tel: (0342) 717707
Dozens of fairground entertainments to hire and book

Regulations

Gaming Board of Great Britain
Berkshire House, 168-173 High Holborn,
London WC1V 7AA
Tel: 071 240 0821
Advice and registration for all forms of lotteries

Customs and Excise
New Kings Beam House 22 Upper Ground,
London SE1 9PJ
Tel: 071 620 1313
Advice on VAT or your local office

The Performing Rights Society Ltd
29-33 Berners Street, London W1P 4AA
Tel: 071 580 5544
Advice on fees that may be payable for live music.

Infrastructure

RAC Signs Service
RAC House, M1 Cross,
Brent Terrace, London NW2 1LT
Tel: 0800 234810 (Freephone)
Highway signs and planning permission

AA Signs Service
Fanum House, Dogkennel Lane,
Halesowen, West Midlands B63 3BT
Tel: 021 501
Highway signs and planning permission

Event Services Ltd
The Old Foundry, Brow Mills Road,
Hipperholme, Halifax,
West Yorkshire HX3 8BZ
Tel: 0422 204114
Complete event infrastructure

GKN Quickform (Birmingham)
Tel: 021 7063399 for your nearest office
Crowd control barriers and fencing

SGB Readyfence
Tel: 081 628 3400 for your nearest office
All types of temporary fencing

The Amazing Bunting Company
PO Box 274, Northampton NN3 4AD
Tel: 0604 786655
As stated, bunting and other types of bazaar and fair equipment

Restroom Rentals / The Search Group
Tel: 0532 639081 for your nearest office
Lavatories

Pilot Hire Ltd
Wimpey Estate, Lancaster Road,
Southall, Middlesex UB1 1NR
Tel: 081 574 3882
Lavatories including disabled facilities

Nipperbout
84 Clonmell Road, London N17 6JU
Tel: 081 801 0148
Mobile creche / childcare

Publicity

Ticketshop
13 Cremyll Road, Reading,
Berkshire RG1 8NQ
Tel: 0734 599234
Official tickets and publicity

Geerings of Ashford Ltd
Cobbs Wood House, Chart Road,
Ashford, Kent TN23 1EP
Tel: 0233 633366
Full publicity service including catalogues and schedules

A few funding sources

Arts Council of Great Britain
14 Great Peter Street,
London SW1P 3NQ
Tel: 071 333 0100

Arts Council of Northern Ireland
185 Stranmillis Road, Belfast,
Northern Ireland BT9 5DU
Tel: 0232 381591

Crafts Council
44a Pentonville Road, Islington,
London N1 9BY
Tel: 071 278 7700

Gulbenkian Foundation
98 Portland Place, London W1N 4ET
Tel: 071 636 5313

London Chamber of Commerce and Industry
69 Cannon Street,
London EC4N 5AB
Tel: 071 248 4444

The Sports Council for England
16 Upper Woburn Place,
London WC1H 0QP.
Tel: 071 383 5740

Charitable information

Central Register of Charities
St. Alban's House, 57/60 Haymarket,
London SW1Y 4QX
Tel: 071 210 3000
Register of all charities

Charity Commission
St Alban's House, 57/60 Haymarket,
London SW1Y 4QX
Tel: 071 210 4405
Advice and numerous leaflets on all charitable concerns

Charities Aid Foundation
48 Pembury Road, Tonbridge,
Kent TN9 2JD
Tel: (07327) 713333
More charity advice

National Federation of Women's Institutes
104 New King's Road,
London SW6 4LY
Tel: 071 371 9300
Information on local groups

Other sources of help

The National Outdoor Events Association,
7 Hamilton Way, Wallington,
Surrey SM6 9NJ
Tel: 081 669 8121
May help with all aspects of events, especially large shows. Sort of entertainments business watchdog.

National Council for Voluntary Organisations
Regent's Warf, All Saint's Street,
London N1 9RL
Tel: 071 713 6161